Tax Tips and Tax Dodges

Tax Tips and Tax Dodges

What You Should and Shouldn't Do to Cut Your Taxes

Edited by Frederick Andrews

DJ
DOW JONES BOOKS
PRINCETON, NEW JERSEY

Manufactured in the United States of America
International Standard Book Number: 0-87128-469-3
Library of Congress card number: 72-179064

Introduction

THIS book will teach you a lot about taxes. If used properly, it should help you cut your tax bill. Whether it does or not, it will tell you how others cut their taxes, or try to. You may consider that a matter of indifference, but as others pay less, you pay more.

The volume is no ordinary tax guide. It doesn't merely describe hypothetical tax situations. Rather, it deals with real conflict and controversy over taxes—with actual borderline cases where taxpayers have won bigger deductions or lower tax rates by going to court. This book gives the specifics, and where names are of interest, it gives the names. In addition to legal decisions, the book also provides the latest interpretations by the Internal Revenue Service of many particular tax questions.

The selections are drawn from the "Tax Report," the popular Page One column published weekly in The Wall Street Journal, the national business daily. Now, for the first time, the best of these weekly columns have been gathered together.

The book has a two-fold purpose. The first is to tell you about tax developments that may save you money by answering questions like these:

—If you get married, will your taxes go down?

—You work at home evenings, but you aren't required to. May you take deductions for your "office" at home?

—Commuting isn't deductible: No tax rule is stricter, but there's one clear exception. What is it?

—You are at odds with the IRS. Can you appeal to a court without incurring expensive legal fees?

—You are a tax cheat, and the IRS has caught up with you. Should you cooperate?

The book is also intended to deepen your understanding of what the tax system is and how it works. In fiscal 1970, the Internal Revenue Service collected no less than $195,722,096,497. The great bulk of this sum came from individuals and businesses who voluntarily paid what was due under the law. As every IRS Commissioner reminds us, our willing compliance is an essential part of the tax system. But at the same time, hundreds of thousands of highly-trained lawyers, accountants and tax advisers make a handsome living counseling clients how to avoid (at times, how to evade) the tax bite. That's part of our tax system, too.

Taxes are more than the government's prime means of raising revenue. They seep into every corner of our life. Rationally applied, taxes may also be a powerful instrument for influencing economic behavior, short of direct controls. When President Nixon sought to shake up a demoralized, lackluster economy, it was only natural that he reached for the investment tax credit.

Taxes are also the end-product of a continual struggle not to pay them—or, rather, to have some groups pay more and others less. Not all classes, industries, interests, or areas are equal in this struggle, or equally well represented when tax laws are made. The Internal Revenue Code may perhaps be classed among the wonders of the modern world. It combines some of the most complex formulations of the human mind with elemental avarice.

The book offers tax tips, not exhaustive answers. It isn't a guide to the 1040 form. The book deals with novel and unsettled areas of tax law. Many (perhaps most) tax questions are well-settled and thus somewhat underrepresented in this book.

The selections were printed in the "Tax Report" during 1969, 1970, and 1971. We have excluded items that later developments have made clearly out-of-date.

Of those included, however, only rarely have items been reworded merely to reflect the passing of time.

We give the original date with every item. With most items, we also give a citation to the underlying court decision or IRS ruling. We urge you to follow these citations to the full texts. These brief tax summaries are as accurate as we can make them, but they necessarily omit many details. One of the omissions may be a detail that makes the precedent unsuited to your circumstances.

A decision that stands as we go to press may later be reversed by a higher court or overridden by a new tax law. The citation should also help you check whether an item is still up-to-date. When a substantial amount of money is involved, there's no substitute for professional tax advice.

The abbreviations "T.C." and "T.C. Memo." refer to the regular and memorandum decisions of the United States Tax Court. The full text of these decisions can be found in *Tax Court Reporter* and *Tax Court Memorandum Decisions,* two legal series published by Commerce Clearing House Inc. Decisions of other federal courts appear in *U.S. Tax Cases,* also published by Commerce Clearing House. Similar legal publications carry the IRS Rulings, which can also be checked at IRS offices.

—FREDERICK ANDREWS
Editor, Tax Report

Contents

Tax Tips and Tax Dodges

Life Is Very Taxing These Days (I)

Who could oppose mother, God, and country? You'd be surprised.

In California, William T. Bagley, chairman of the state assembly's revenue committee, became irked by incessant pleas for special tax consideration. He offered his own measure, which asked an exemption from sales tax for "white canes for the blind, Bibles, the United States flag and Mother's Day cards."

The bill was meant as a wry attempt at "legislative enlightment," Bagley says, but it isn't clear how much light is being shed. One legislator suggested a $10 tax credit for anyone who bought a flag. (It would be cheaper to give every Californian a flag, Bagley retorted.) Then a minister objected to favoritism for religion and asked equal treatment for Darwin. Even the blind complained that they don't need special treatment.

Nothing's been said about the Mother's Day cards. "Everybody's in favor of motherhood," says a Bagley aide. But no one's heard from the population people.

5/27/70

Marriage and Joint Returns

Wages of sin? A working couple is taxed less unwed than wed, a study says.

"If you must work, don't marry; if you must marry, don't work." That's the conclusion of an article in Taxes magazine that spells out the impact of "tax reform" changes on a man and wife who both work. The author, Britt Richards, contends that raising the standard deduction and personal exemption and lowering rates on single persons results in a hefty "marriage penalty" on a working couple.

In 1970, he says, if husband and wife earn $14,000 apiece, together they will pay $360 more in Federal income taxes than a similar couple without benefit of wedlock. By 1972, as tax changes are phased in, the difference will rise to $972. Even if one partner's earnings are much greater than the other's, a similar (though smaller) penalty results. In the view of Mr. Richards, who is married, the notion of the joint return is rooted in inequity. It allows a husband and wife to split their income, but it really benefits only the single-income family, he contends.

"It assumes that marriage takes only one form," he asserts. "The husband goes off to work, kisses his wife at the door, and returns in the evening to hear about her day's activities with the garden club."

5/6/70

His-or-Her brokerage accounts face a joint bank account test, the IRS rules.

Many married couples set up joint brokerage accounts, with right of survivorships, even though one partner provides all the money to buy securities. Under the arrangement, the broker will accept instructions from either joint owner or turn over the holdings to either one. Often, stocks are held in a "street" name, commonly that of the brokerage house.

Until recently, the IRS has been silent on the tax consequences of street-name joint accounts. Now it has published a ruling based on its previous stance on joint bank accounts. A husband may put up the cash to buy stock, but as long as the securities stay in the account and he can reclaim them without his wife's consent, no gift results. But if his wife draws on the account for her benefit, what she withdraws is a gift, for Federal gift tax purposes.

(Rev. Ruling 69-148.)
4/9/69

Check, Check-Mate: A domestic drama in two acts:

A married taxpayer filed a joint return for 1965 without his wife's knowledge. (All the income on the return was his.) Then, in 1968, the IRS sent the couple a notice of deficiency for $2,154. The man petitioned the Tax Court in protest, but he also sent the IRS a check for an additional $954. The IRS records, however, didn't show that he owed anything for 1965 (apparently because the deficiency claim was still pending), so the IRS returned the $954 as a refund.

By this time, the couple was divorced, and the $954 refund check went to the ex-wife's address. She cashed the check, after endorsing it with both her former husband's name and her own. The man protested that he never received the refund, but the Tax Court ruled he did. It cited the wife's testimony that she telephoned him about the check, but he told her he didn't want to be bothered with her and she should keep it. The ex-husband never challenged this testimony, the Tax Court said.

His statement "might reasonably be interpreted" as an authorization to sign his name and cash the check, the Tax Court decided. Thus, the man constructively received the refund, it ruled.

(Wiener v. Commissioner, T.C. Memo. 1971-56.)
4/7/71

Wedlocked: In several cases, women who signed joint returns were later dunned for taxes on money their husbands stole, though they had no part in it. Now a wife has been ruled liable for taxes the IRS couldn't extract from her spouse on money he earned abroad. The couple originally filed a joint return. They assumed the $10,150 he earned in Vietnam would be tax-exempt but he re-entered the U.S. too soon. The Tax Court wouldn't allow the wife to file an amended separate return. This ruling created "unfairness, (but) we see no escape from this unfortunate result."

(Wilson v. Commissioner, T.C. Memo. 1970-105.)
5/13/70

Gross fears the tax bill might reward a "friendly divorce," but Mills is dubious.

Combatants in the fight over tax revisions are digging in for a long winter. But the Senate debate will be hard put to top this House exchange over a cut in tax rates on single persons 35 or over. Rep. Gross asked whether a married couple over 34 might not do better if they managed a friendly divorce, split their income between them, but continued to live together:

Mr. Mills: If the (IRS) agent found out about it in a state recognizing common law marriages, I would think they would be treated as married for tax purposes.

Mr. Gross: Does the gentleman from Arkansas have

a provision in this bill for a man in the house?

Mr. Mills: No; the bill does not. . . .

Mr. Gross: Or a man in the woodshed? . . . Or a man under the bed?

Mr. Mills: We discussed all those factors when we had the matter of welfare payments before us in 1967. This does not involve the welfare program. . . .

Mr. Gross: If I could induce my wife to enter into this sort of agreement, it seems to me it would be real welfare.

Mr. Mills: The gentleman is a very persuasive man, but knowing his wife as I do, I know he will never persuade her.

9/24/69

A Montana man filed a joint return, but his wife never signed it. Instead, the husband jotted on the return, "Wife away caring for ailing mother." The IRS contended the return wasn't a joint return, and it dunned the husband at higher single-taxpayer rates. The Tax Court disagreed. If both spouses show that they meant a return to be joint when it was filed, then the lack of one signature doesn't matter, the court said.

(Hill v. Commissioner, T.C. Memo. 1971-127.)
6/16/71

No fraud results merely because a husband doesn't tell all about a joint return.

That's the latest Tax Court decision in a painful, difficult case. Back in 1968, it ruled, reluctantly, that because a woman signed a joint return, she was liable for taxes due on $100,000 her husband embezzled (without her knowledge). Last year an appeals court disagreed. It ordered the Tax Court to look at the circumstances of her signing the return. It ruled that some factors—duress, signing by mistake, trickery or fraud—could wipe out the signature.

The Tax Court took a second look, but found no extenuating circumstances. The husband never threatened or forced her to sign, or even said the returns were accurate. He didn't bother to forge her name because he knew she would sign. (She felt she ought to "mind her husband," she said.) In this context, the court held that his keeping mum about not reporting the embezzled funds wasn't fraud.

"To hold that such nondisclosure rises to the level of fraud would open a Pandora's box to avoidance of liability on joint returns," the court declared.

(Huelsman v. Commissioner, 54 T.C. No. 135.)

7/8/70

A new law shields an innocent wife from being held accountable for her husband's tax frauds. In one case, because a woman had signed a joint return, she was held liable for taxes due on $100,000 her husband embezzled. The new act, signed by President Nixon, provides that a spouse who isn't a party to fraudulent omission of income from a tax return won't be liable. The provision won't be applied, however, unless the omission is more than 25% of the total income reported.

1/20/71

Claiming a Dependent

Fine points in claiming a parent as a dependent come out in a Tax Court case.

To claim a dependent, one must provide more than half of his or her support. A Texas man recently met this test for his elderly grandmother, even though she received $942 in old-age benefits and $70 in Medicare-Medicaid premiums from the state of Texas. The IRS claimed that this $1,012 total exceeded the $915 that the grandson said he provided in food, lodging, utilities, laundry and transportation.

The Tax Court nevertheless ruled for the grandson because not everything the grandmother got from the state was spent on her support. She spent $19 on burial insurance and gave $60 more to her son—neither item considered "support." That narrowed the gap between the state's contribution and her grandson's to $18. And he provided more transportation, and she gave away a few more dollars, than was precisely claimed, the court decided. These items tipped the scales for the grandson.

This was another case in which a taxpayer represented himself before the Tax Court. "Petitioner was forthright and truthful. We find no reason to doubt him," the court said.

(Carter v. Commissioner, 55 T.C. No. 13.)
11/4/70

The IRS proposes new rules for divorced parents in claiming dependents.

To claim a child as a dependent, one must provide more than half his support. In divorces or separations, that's often hard to prove, especially when the parents are at odds. Last week the IRS proposed new regulations to implement a 1967 law. They generally assume that the parent with custody of the child may claim him or her as a dependent, but they propose two important exceptions.

First, if the divorce decree provides, or the parents agree, that the "noncustodial" parent (usually the father) may claim the dependent, the IRS will accept that as long as he gives at least $600 a year in support. Secondly, whatever the divorce terms, if the noncustodial parent pays $1,200 or more in support his outlays will be presumed to provide more than half unless the custodial parent (the mother) clearly shows otherwise.

The IRS would also entitle either parent to get from the other an itemized statement of the support that parent provides. The parent asking the itemization must give a similar statement in exchange.

(Notice of Proposed Rule Making, Federal Register, Sept. 12, 1970.)
9/23/70

Another court rules that head-of-household means more than token occupancy.

The Fourth Circuit has reversed a lower court decision that gave head-of-household tax status to an unmarried South Carolina man. The man supported his two elderly sisters, who lived in the old home place. The taxpayer kept a room and a few things there, but actually lived in a nearby town. The district court said he had always considered the old place "one of his homes," and "token or implied occupancy" was enough.

But the Fourth Circuit disagreed. It quotes legislative history specifying that the household be the taxpayer's "actual place of abode." (This doesn't apply to taxpayers who maintain homes for their parents.) The household needn't be his principal place of abode, but "it must be his home, where he and the other members of the household live together for a substantial part of the time," the circuit court said.

The decision accords with previous decisions in the Fifth and Seventh circuits. But the Ninth Circuit has ruled otherwise.

(Muse v. U.S.A., U.S. Ct. of Appeals, 4th Cir., 1970.)
11/25/70

Supporting a parent in a rest home or home for the aged may become less expensive. An IRS ruling has conceded that an unmarried taxpayer who furnishes such support qualifies for head-of-household tax rates. Normally a single taxpayer who pays more than half the costs of his parent's household is a head-of-household, but the IRS has long argued that a room in a rest home doesn't amount to a household. Both the Tax Court and a circuit court have rejected this argument.

(Rev. Ruling 70-279.)
6/19/70

Foster children may be claimed as dependents under the same rules that apply to natural and adopted children, according to proposed IRS regulations. They define a foster child as one "in the case of a person or persons (other than parents or adopted parents) who care for the child as their own." The proposed regulations implement the Tax Reform Act.

4/22/70

Living proof: A divorced woman won the right to claim her four children, ages 8 to 15, as dependents even though her former husband gave $3,900 a year toward their support. The woman demonstrated that she provided more than half their support. She submitted a table of annual expenses that totaled $8,670, including $600 or $700 a child for food. "Although the amounts estimated for food seem a little high," the Tax Court said, "we had occasion to observe the boys at trial. Their size attests to the hearty appetites"—and the food costs.

(Herbert v. Commissioner, T.C. Memo. 1970-216.)
8/5/70

A divorced father beat the IRS and won the right to claim his two sons as dependents. The IRS didn't contest the $2,500 he spent on the boys (who lived with their mother), but it claimed the father didn't prove he provided half their support. The Tax Court said he didn't have to show the exact amount of their total support, but merely show "by sufficient and cogent evidence" that he contributed more than half. This he did through testimony about their scale of living and the limited earning capacity of his former wife.

(Hyde v. Commissioner, T.C. Memo. 1970-256.)
9/16/70

"Mens sana in corpore sano," the Tax Court declared in a camp opinion: A sound mind in a sound body. That dictum popped up in a dispute over who could claim a young boy as a dependent. His divorced mother had provided more than half his support if $917 for eight weeks at summer camp in Maine was counted. The IRS found the fee "preposterous" and argued that "support" meant the "necessities of life." But the court "completely disagreed" with so narrow a definition. Camp benefited the boy's development, it said.

(Shapiro v. Commissioner, 54 T.C. No. 31.)
3/4/70

Child care expenses, within limits, may be deducted by a woman or a widower, provided the purpose is to allow the taxpayer to be gainfully employed. But a twist in the law often denies a mother the deduction if she is divorced. Recently, for example, the Tax Court ruled against a divorcee who claimed a $709 child-care deduction. To qualify, the court said, the children must be her dependents, and—as is frequently the case—her former husband's support payments entitled him, not her, to claim the dependents.

(Bosher v. Commissioner, T.C. Memo. 1971-10.)
1/27/71

Maybe Uncle Sam can claim this deduction: When a California man underwent surgery, his illness cost his son $2,400 in medical bills, but the younger man gained no tax relief. He couldn't deduct the medical outlays because his father wasn't his dependent. And that was because the elderly man also received $3,000 from Social Security and government welfare agencies. The son argued vainly before the Tax Court that such nontaxable income shouldn't count. In plain English, a dependent must get "over half of his support from the taxpayer," the court recited.

(Beck v. Commissioner, T.C. Memo. 1970-153.)
6/24/70

A divorced woman recently raised a novel tax claim. She argued that the IRS violated the Ninth Amendment by checking whether she (rather than her former husband) could claim their children as dependents. The amendment states that the enumeration of certain constitutional rights shouldn't be construed as denying the existence of others. The IRS violated her privacy by intruding into "unpleasant personal, domestic affairs," she said. A sincere plea, but "legally unsound," the Tax Court ruled.

(Campbell v. Commissioner, T.C. Memo. 1971-51.)
3/31/71

A New York woman claimed her elderly mother as a dependent on the ground that, aside from Social Security, the mother earned less than $600 a year. She received a pension of $50 a month, but one month $8 was deducted as a death-benefit payment, netting her $592 for the year. The Tax Court ruled she had earned $600, however. It was the same as receiving $600 and paying the $8 out-of-pocket.

(Carito v. Commissioner, 54 T.C. No. 157.)
8/26/70

Sour grapes: Some bachelors in Cleveland write that they had heady dreams of making their own wine. Thousands of amateur vintners take advantage of a Federal law allowing them to turn out up to 200 gallons a year, tax-free, for their own consumption. But the bachelors' vision went flat, they say. The Treasury told them the exception is open by law only to heads of households, and bachelors don't qualify. "A most unusual and probably unconstitutional law," one single fellow says.

9/23/70

Taxes and Alimony

A liberated idea of support for a former wife is taxed as plain ol' alimony.

In Texas, a divorced woman didn't ask "alimony," but her former husband agreed to pay her way through law school to help her become self-supporting. The woman claimed he was discharging "a moral obligation" because she had worked while he went to school. And under Texas law, she contended, he wasn't obliged to educate his former wife.

But the IRS called it alimony and taxed it as such. The Tax Court recently agreed. If the former husband undertook a legal obligation to make payments, and the obligation had all the earmarks of alimony, then the alimony tax rules apply, the court said. It made no difference that he did more than the law required.

(Kern v. Commissioner, 55 T.C. No. 40.)
12/16/70

Some marriages are made in Heaven, but others aren't.

Here's an odd one for you: A twice-married woman was collecting $23,000 a year in alimony from Husband No. 2. Somehow Husband No. 2 wasn't invited to wedding No. 3, perhaps because he was entitled to cut off the gravy if his former wife remarried. Husband No. 3 later testified that keeping things quiet was his wife's idea; she claimed it was his. In any event, she collected an extra $23,000 before Husband No. 2 caught on. He obtained a judgment that she pay it back as "unjust enrichment."

The couple also neglected to mention the $23,000 to the IRS. Later, Husband No. 3 contended the sum wasn't taxable as alimony because No. 2 hadn't been legally obliged to pay it. The money must have been a tax-free gift or loan. The Tax Court thought that calling it a gift was stretching things. In addition, it said, the wife's obligation to repay the sum didn't mean it wasn't income. Her obligation, it declared, was "not in substance different" from an embezzler's, whose embezzlement is taxable even though the law requires that he pay the money back.

By the time the case reached court, Husband No. 3 was simply Former No. 3. But the court held him liable for taxes on the entire $23,000 because he knew of the omission when he signed the joint return.

(Joss v. Commissioner, 56 T.C. No. 27.)
6/2/71

Insurance premiums as alimony payments are clarified by an IRS ruling.

The ruling concerned a divorced man who took out two policies on his life. The first he irrevocably assigned to his ex-wife, with her as beneficiary and their children as beneficiaries in the event of her death. The second policy named the children as beneficiaries and the former wife as next in line.

Premiums on the first policy qualified as alimony deductions and were income for the woman, the IRS ruled. That's because the arrangement was part of a court-approved settlement, and the man signed over the policy for good. The second policy, however, was voluntary, and he retained control of it. Thus it was neither alimony nor otherwise deductible.

(Rev. Ruling 70-218.)
5/13/70

A deal's a deal, an appeals court says, and it upholds a good-faith compromise.

In 1944, a GI divorced his wife, who had left him,

and she soon married again. He heard nothing more for 20 years, until he was about to sell some land for $322,-350. The buyer questioned the original divorce and required that the woman sign a release. This she happily did—for $40,000 in cash and land. She claimed the sum was paid for release of her dower rights, but the IRS and the Tax Court called it taxable income. If the divorce was valid—and they weren't convinced it wasn't—she had no dower rights to give up, they said.

The Fifth Circuit Appeals Court recently toppled that decision and sided with the woman. The key point, it said, wasn't whether the divorce was valid, but rather whether the woman had good reasons to think it wasn't and entered a "good faith compromise" of her rights. Society has a stake in the peaceful settlement of disputes, the court said, and thus "there are strong policy reasons for taking at face value compromises based on claims made in good faith."

Nor had the woman waited too long to question the divorce. No one had been clearly injured by the delay, the court said.

(Howard v. Commissioner, U.S. Ct. of Appeals, 5th Cir., 1971.)
6/16/71

An Illinois woman didn't have to pay taxes on support payments from her former husband, the Tax Court rules. Federal law says a divorced woman's gross income includes payments received under "a legal obligation . . . imposed on or incurred by the husband." But in this case, the woman married again, and even though her first husband continued to pay her support, he had no legal obligation under Illinois law to do so.

(Hoffman v. Commissioner, 54 T.C. No. 156.)
8/19/70

Tax-free alimony was upheld by a U.S. circuit court in a recent case. The ruling concerned a woman who benefited from an alimony trust set up by her former husband. Normally alimony is taxable, but part of the trust holdings was tax-exempt bonds. The court ruled that a like portion of her payments were tax-exempt. Under standard "conduit" rules applied to trusts, income keeps its original exempt character in the hands of a beneficiary.

(Ellis v. U.S.A., U.S. Ct. of Appeals, 6th Cir., 1969.)
10/22/69

Is It Income?

Ford leases bargain Continentals to Congressmen —but is the bargain taxable?

This week United Press International detailed how Ford Motor Co. leases its luxury cars to at least 19 ranking Congressmen for $750 a year. You or I would have to pay about $3,480 to lease similar splendor. Ford says the preferential arrangement is part of a policy of putting its cars in the hands of prestigious drivers. But tax lawyers say there's some question whether the $2,730 saving is a tax-free gift or taxable income for the Congressmen.

The IRS says it hasn't ruled on the point. But back in 1962, Ford provided Paul Hornung, the football star, with free use of a Thunderbird. The Tax Court ruled Hornung had to pay taxes on its $600 rental value. It said Ford enjoyed "the intangible benefits of (Hornung's) implied personal endorsement." A gift springs from "detached and disinterested generosity . . . affection, admiration (or) charity."

Maybe Ford feels that way about football stars and Congressmen. In Hornung's case, "it seems more likely that (Ford) believed football stars would (help) the sales image of Thunderbirds," the court said.

(Hornung v. Commissioner, 47 T.C. No. 42.)
8/5/70

"Oh fiddlesticks!" Sen. Cotton says: It'd be "absurd" to tax his bargain auto lease.

Congressmen and Senators who enjoy slashed-rate leases on Continentals say it never entered their heads that their saving could be considered taxable income. Many say the only tax treatment they give the matter is to deduct their $750 rental as a business expense—and not all of them do that. Sen. Cotton disputes the $3,480 quoted as the normal cost of leasing a Continental for a year. "You'd have to be an awful simpleton to pay that amount."

A number of lawmakers say the preferential leases have gone on for years without being questioned. "I'm a former Internal Revenue man, and it isn't a gift," Rep. Dulski (D., N.Y.) asserts. "It's a contract between Ford and myself. A deductible item. I checked with IRS." Rep. Poage (D., Texas) has "absolutely no comment."

8/5/70

The IRS stiffens its line on scholarship aid tied to future employment.

In fields where qualified people are scarce, a public agency will sometimes give college scholarships to students who promise to work for the agency after graduation. Such aid hasn't been considered taxable income for the recipient. Now, however, the IRS says it will no longer abide by the leading precedent on the point, a 1960 Tax Court decision involving a girl who went through nursing school under such an arrangement with the State of Tennessee.

The IRS is basing its turnabout on a Supreme Court decision last year. The High Court ruled that what Westinghouse paid an employe on leave of absence in graduate school was taxable income. (He had agreed to return to Westinghouse for at least two years.) Prior employment with the donor really doesn't matter, the IRS contends. The key point is whether a stipend is "granted to return for the quid pro quo of a promise to render future services."

Internal Revenue says it won't apply its new stance to stipends received prior to June 30, 1970.

(Rev. Ruling 70-283.)
6/17/70

Medicare benefits aren't income, but they may count as support, the IRS says.

Last week the IRS spelled out the tax standing of Medicare. Basic Medicare benefits—financed by payroll taxes and open to almost all elderly persons—are legally the same as Social Security, the IRS says, and thus not taxable. Supplementary Medicare, which covers only those who enroll and pay a monthly premium, isn't taxable, either, but for a different reason: It's treated like proceeds from private health and accident insurance, which generally aren't considered income.

But Medicare may affect an elderly person's status as a dependent, the IRS says. To claim someone as a dependent, a taxpayer must provide over half his total support. Basic Medicare benefits will be counted as support the recipient provides himself. The supplementary benefits won't constitute support, the IRS says, but the premiums paid will be support provided by whoever pays them.

The IRS also says that Medicare benefits aren't included in computing the limit on the income tax credit elderly persons already enjoy on retirement income.

(Rev. Ruling 70-341.)
7/15/70

An executive died, and his company wanted to "do something" for his widow.

It was a young company, and the man was the first of its principals to die. The firm voted to give his widow $25,000 plus her late husband's company car. Was all this a gift or income? A jury decided the transfer was a tax-free gift. The IRS asked an appeals court to set the verdict aside, but the court refused.

In theory, a gift is motivated by "detached and disinterested generosity." There are so many shadings in practice, however, that "each case must be treated individually," the court declared. For instance, a payment to express gratitude for an employe's services, without regard for his widow's needs, is considered income. So is a payment mainly intended to assure surviving executives that the company is a good place to work. In the present case, the company's only possible self-serving motive would be to show that it "takes care of its own," the court said.

Had it been the jury, the court declared, it would have ruled for the IRS. But it decided "reasonable people" could have found that "natural sympathy and concern" were the firm's motive. Thus the court let the verdict stand.

(Grinstead v. U.S.A., U.S. Ct. of Appeals, 7th Cir., 1971.)
8/11/71

Tip income causes problems for some wage earners.

There's no question that tips are taxable payment for services and not gifts, but this hasn't prevented all sorts of tax difficulties for waiters and others who fail to keep an accurate record of such income.

In one recent case, a San Francisco beautician reported receiving $575 in tips during 1965. But on the basis of the employer's records, the IRS figured the man's average tip was 8% for his services which raised the amount of tips to $2,250. Since the beautician kept no records of his own, the Tax Court agreed that he should ante up another $741 in taxes. It was a bit harder for the IRS to figure the tax deficiencies for three Salt Lake City waitresses who didn't keep records but reported tip income equal to about 3% of their total checks during the year. After studying the operation of the restaurant, the Revenue Service figured the average tip was 11%, but adjusted that to 8% since some 25% of patrons didn't tip at all and part of the tip money was passed along to bus boys.

The Tax Court went a little easier on the waitresses. It agreed with the IRS' method of computing their income but decided the average tip was only 8%. This lowered the adjusted tip income to 5¾% of sales.

(Becerra v. Commissioner, T.C. Memo. 1969-22
Hills et al. v. Commissioner, T.C. Memo. 1968-293.)
2/12/69

What new partners pay to join a practice may qualify as capital gain.

The IRS has backed away from a previous position it took despite some court decisions to the contrary. Until last week it held that when a lawyer, doctor or other professional admitted a new partner to his firm, the newcomer was buying a share in the firm's future earnings. Thus what he paid was taxable as ordinary income to the original partner or partners.

The Revenue Service refused to recognize any part of the sum as a payment for goodwill. It argued that unless the firm changed hands entirely, the original partners, remaining in practice, continued to benefit from goodwill. Now, however, it concedes that a partial transfer of goodwill may in fact be involved when a new partner enters a firm. A payment for such goodwill is a capital gain for the seller.

The IRS says such transactions "will be carefully scrutinized to assure that goodwill in fact exists." The new ruling doesn't give details on the criteria to be applied.

(Rev. Ruling 70-45.)
2/11/70

A dealer's hand didn't spoil a capital gain for fellow real estate investors.

A real estate dealer organized a group of individual investors to join him in buying an interest in an unimproved tract. When the dealer subsequently sold his share to another group member, his profit was taxed as ordinary income, because of his dealer status. Later, the remaining participants sold the property. The Treasury sought to tax their gain as ordinary income, too.

In this case, a U.S. Court of Appeals demurred. Teaming up with a dealer didn't necessarily transform his partners into pros, the court said. Not all who take part in a joint venture need have the same intent and purpose. For some, the court noted, the transaction may be a routine step in their business; but for others, merely a single investment opportunity with a view to ultimate profit. The individual investors' profits were capital gains, the court ruled.

(Riddell v. Scales, U.S. Ct. of Appeals, 9th Cir., 1969.)
2/26/69

Strike benefits are taxable income, a jury in Tennessee decides.

Lawyers say the Supreme Court hasn't laid down a clear-cut rule on whether strike payments are taxable. Union members have argued that such payments are gifts and thus tax-free. Recently, a district court jury rejected this argument, however, in a case that grew out of the prolonged strike against Kingsport Press Inc. From April 1963 until December 1965, the taxpayer received $50 a week from his union. Of the $7,350 total, the union was legally bound to pay only $400.

To get strike benefits, the taxpayer was required to sign in daily with the union. In addition, if he got an outside job, or turned down one, he became ineligible. According to the judge, the key issue was whether the union acted "purely out of respect, of charity, of good will." If the union hoped to spur the taxpayer to stay on strike, the payments weren't a gift, the judge instructed the jury.

One union lawyer still chafes for a decisive ruling on taxability. "It's absurd to leave an issue like this to a jury," he declares.

(McConnell v. U.S.A., U.S. Dist. Ct., East. Dist. Tenn., 1970.)
7/1/70

Maury Wills claims artistry in stealing bases, but an appeals court cuts him down.

It recently upheld a Tax Court decision that dealt with awards Wills won in 1962, the year the Dodger star smashed all base-stealing records. The appeals court ruled that Wills, now with the Montreal Expos, had to pay taxes on the $1,700 MG he won as "most popular Dodger" and the S. Rae Hickok belt, worth about $8,-000, as outstanding pro athlete of 1962. By law, prizes are normally taxed, but there are exceptions for "artistic, literary or civic achievement." But the circuit court turned an umpire's eye to Wills' contention that his base-line thefts qualified for the exception.

The court also denied the ballplayer's claim that the Hickok belt shouldn't be taxed because it was a trophy, rather than a useful prize like the car. The belt could be sold, the court noted, and thus was the equivalent of cash.

"The law requires the foregoing conclusion," the court added with distaste. "We are convinced that it is an inequitable result. The next step would be to tax the gold and silver in Olympic medals."

(Wills v. Commissioner, U.S. Ct. of Appeals, 9th Cir., 1969.)
5/28/69

There's no quid pro quo in a football scholarship—or so the Tax Court says.

Back in 1965, James Heidel, a University of Mississippi football star, was given a $50,000 bonus when he signed with the St. Louis Cardinals. Recently, Heidel was in Tax Court, claiming the right to average his 1965 income, including the $50,000, over 1961-65. The IRS had balked, contending that he hadn't provided 50% or more of his own support each year during the five-year period, as tax law normally requires. At issue was 1961, when Heidel earned $716, his parents provided $964, and $657 came from an Ole Miss football scholarship.

Heidel said the $657 was support he provided for himself because he had to play football to keep the scholarship. But the Tax Court wouldn't go along. If Ole Miss required services in return, the grant would have to be taxable income, the court declared. It would be "more consistent with the ordinary understanding" of an athletic scholarship to rule the $657 wasn't support Heidel provided for himself, the court concluded.

Heidel also argued the $50,000 was attributable to "work" performed in 1963 and 1964. But the court said he was paid to sign, not to reward him for his play.

(Heidel v. Commissioner, 56 T.C. No. 10.)
4/28/71

The salad days of the Great Salad Oil Swindle left an incredible tax tangle.

A lot of cash changed hands before the bubble burst in 1963 for Allied Crude Vegetable Oil Refining Corp. Ever since, the IRS has been trying to figure who owed taxes on what. The latest court case involves Lillian Pascarelli, who "lived as husband and wife" with Anthony DeAngelis, the Tax Court found. (DeAngelis was convicted in 1965 of interstate transportation of forged warehouse receipts.)

The case involved $202,000 Mrs. Pascarelli received from DeAngelis over five years, plus $32,406 he put into a commodity account in her name. Mrs. Pascarelli claimed she merely held the assets for DeAngelis, despite a documented record of expenditures of her own. The IRS argued that the money was pay for services rendered in helping DeAngelis to entertain business friends. If that wasn't so, the IRS said, then the transfers were gifts.

The Tax Court found the money was indeed a gift, prompted by "love and affection and disinterested generosity." But it held Mrs. Pascarelli liable for gift taxes because DeAngelis hadn't paid them.

(Pascarelli v. Commissioner, 55 T.C. No. 100.)
3/31/71

Miss America finds a court unimpressed by her efforts to win the crown.

Deborah Bryant Wilson, Miss America of 1966, lost her claim to average her hefty title-year earnings over five years for tax purposes. To qualify for averaging under the special "major accomplishment" rule, she had to show that more than half of her 1965-66 income was attributable to work done in at least two previous years. She contended it was because she had entered beauty contests and taken courses in modeling and dramatics, all with an eye to the Miss America crown.

Such efforts may have made her Miss America, a district court conceded, but they weren't what the tax code meant by work. Winning the Miss America title merely gave her the chance to make some money, the court said; the actual income came from appearances for pageant sponsors like Oldsmobile. All that was done in her reign, not before.

(Wilson v. U.S.A., U.S. Dist. Ct., Dist. Kansas, 1971.)
2/10/71

Former Governor William G. Stratton of Illinois was upheld in tax-fraud litigation.

The IRS claimed that Stratton's income for 1953-60, the years he was in office, came to $366,000, or $194,000 more than the $172,000 Stratton reported. The IRS used bank accounts and other records to reconstruct how much Stratton's net worth had increased while he was governor. It also levied penalties for under-payment of taxes due to fraud. Stratton had been acquitted of criminal tax fraud.

The Tax Court upheld Stratton, however, and the

main point was the treatment of political contributions. A campaign contribution diverted to personal use becomes taxable income, but an outright gift isn't taxable. In Stratton's case, the court ruled that $43,600 of "unreported income" had been in fact "outright, unrestricted gifts." By the court's reckoning, Stratton had understated his income by only $82,000. But for most of this sum, the statute of limitations had expired because no fraud was proved, the court said.

The bulk of the unreported income came from contributions used for personal ends. But Stratton could have "reasonably believed" these contested sums were gifts.

(Stratton v. Commissioner, 54 T.C. No. 23.)
2/18/70

Sometimes it pays to be small-fry: A court concludes that a rake-off was meager.

Two Massachusetts lawyers (Richard C. Simmers and Richard K. Gordon) were convicted of larceny in a 1960 conspiracy with officials of Foundation Co., New York, to pay a $150,000 bribe in connection with the firm's contract to build a parking garage under Boston Common. Fake legal fees, a dummy corporation and other devices were part of the scheme, during which the two men received $174,000 from Foundation Co. On investigation, the IRS ruled the entire sum was taxable to them.

But the Tax Court accepted the lawyers' protest that they were mere go-betweens in handling $140,000 of the money. The court said they were "small town lawyers," unlikely to receive so large a fee either for legal services or for peddling their non-existent influence. It found that "payment for their services" had been limited to $34,000.

The court conceded that the stories the men related differed from what they had told the IRS earlier. But it decided they had been lying previously, to avoid self-incrimination or reprisals.

(Nunez v. Commissioner, T.C. Memo. 1969-216.)
10/22/69

Note-worthy: A California man served as a financial adviser to a wealthy man, who on one occasion lent him $25,000. The debt was evidenced by a demand note, bearing no interest, on which the lender scribbled, "In case of my death . . . tear up. It's all yours." The lender later died, and his estate acknowledged it had no claim to the sum. The IRS promptly held the $25,000 was income because the estate had forgiven the debt. But the Tax Court ruled the lender had made a gift, even though he could have called the note before he died.

(Bosse v. Commissioner, T.C. Memo. 1970-355.)
1/20/71

A novel tax dodge got short shrift in Tax Court cases involving three Maryland couples. It worked like this: The husband would make deposits in a joint bank account, from which only his wife would make withdrawals, to meet normal living expenses. The wife would put her pay in another account, which only the husband would tap. The taxpayers then claimed the sums thus switched were deductible as gifts. The Tax Court, a bit mystified, could find no such provision in Federal law.

(Laque v. Commissioner, 54 T.C. No. 12.)
2/11/70

Bank giveaways to long-term depositors are interest income and fully taxable in the year received, the IRS rules. Some banks have claimed that gifts like autos and boats, offered in lieu of interest, should be treated as a return of capital and the tax on interest spread over a number of years. But the IRS says the merchandise is interest, taxable when received at its fair market value.

(IRS News Release No. 1032, 1970.)
4/15/70

They laughed when they searched the piano but oh, when they started to pay! An Ohio couple paid $15 for an aged piano, then seven years later found $4,467 in greenbacks inside. The couple paid an $857 income tax on their find, but promptly sued for a refund. Any tax owed was due the year they acquired the piano-and-cash, they argued, and the statute of limitations had since expired. Not so, a U.S. district court ruled. Possession began with discovery, and the sum was taxable that year.

(Cesarini v. U.S.A., U.S. Dist. Ct., No. Dist. Ohio, 1969.)
3/26/69

The Indochina war outpaced the tax law, but now the law is catching up. Yesterday, the Treasury proposed that combat-zone tax benefits apply to military people outside a designated zone, provided their duties support operations in the zone and they qualify for "hostile fire" pay. This would cover men who served in Cambodia, some in Laos, and airmen on combat missions, no matter where based. The benefit exempts enlisted men's pay, and up to $500 a month for officers, from taxes. The change would be retroactive.

(Treasury Dept. News Release, Aug. 4, 1970.)
8/5/70

Uncle Sam spells out what he means by "combat pay." (An enlisted man's pay is tax-exempt if earned in a combat zone, and so is up to $500 a month for officers.) The IRS ruled this week that the exemption also applies to a variety of special payments, including reenlistment bonuses, relocation allowances, pay in lieu of leave, and even cash awards for suggestions. All must be related to combat-zone service as laid down in the IRS ruling.

8/4/71

A Pan Am pilot claimed that $3,500 of his 1968 pay should be tax-free as combat pay because he flew 20 missions in Vietnam, ferrying troops or supplies. Once his airplane was hit by small-arms fire. The Tax Court shot him down. It ruled that the exclusion was limited to persons on active service with the Armed Forces. Whatever the danger, the pilot didn't qualify.

(Fagerland v. Commissioner, T.C. Memo. 1971-134.)
6/16/71

An award paid to the widow of a naval officer killed when Israeli airplanes fired on the U.S.S. Liberty in June 1967, during the Mideast outbreak, didn't have to be included in her income for tax purposes, the IRS held. The award resulted from a claim submitted to the Israeli government by the State Department.

(Rev. Ruling 68-649.)
1/8/69

No bull: In its report on the tax revision bill, the Ways and Means Committee also commented on "an erroneous interpretation of present law." It seems that some cattle-raisers speed the building up of breeding herds by trading off unwanted male calves for female calves in a tax-free "like kind" exchange. That's not what Congress meant by "like kind," the committee said. "The male animals are not held for breeding and, in fact, are not of a 'like kind' with females," it observed.

8/27/69

A bronze sculpture caught the eye of an Ohio couple, who bought it with $7,000 from the funds of their wholly owned small business. The work of art was carried as an investment on the company's books but actually it graced the couple's living room. The couple said they were just holding it, but the Tax Court ruled it a $7,000 dividend. The business never controlled the sculpture, charged them for its use, or invested in any other art.

(Proskauer v. Commissioner, T.C. Memo. 1971-174.)
7/28/71

An insurance man was paid $50,000 to terminate his exclusive general agency contract. He claimed the sum was a capital gain, but a U.S. Circuit Court disagreed. He was giving up the chance to earn commissions, which are taxed as ordinary income. Thus the money he got was also ordinary income, the court held.

(Elliott v. U.S.A., U.S. Ct. of Appeals, 10th Cir., 1970.)
9/2/70

Horse feathers, said a circuit court to a taxpayer who claimed long-term capital gains treatment for insurance proceeds on a colt that died five days after birth. The claimant, who raised racing horses, argued he acquired a property interest in the foal when it was conceived—which, in the nature of things, was more than six months before. He noted he could insure the unborn foal, which he said presumed an insurable interest existed. But an unborn colt wasn't useful property, the appeals court said. The holding period began with birth.

(Greer v. U.S.A., U.S. Ct. of Appeals, 6th Cir., 1969.)
4/2/69

Render unto Caesar: A minister was buying a new house, and it occurred to him to ease the burden by having his entire pay designated a "rental allowance," which by law is tax-free for ministers. It didn't work. The tax-free portion of his pay is limited to the "fair rental value" of his home, plus utilities, the IRS said.

(Rev. Ruling 71-280.)
7/14/71

Is It a Medical Expense?

An invalid at home raises a factual question about what's a medical expense.

When someone is hired to care for an invalid at home, there isn't any hard-and-fast rule about what portion of the expense is deductible as a medical outlay. The tax situation may be especially uncertain when the hired help has no special medical training. The Tax Court recently allowed a Missouri couple a bigger medical deduction than the IRS did, but provided no explicit rationale for doing so.

The man's wife had suffered a series of strokes, which left her unable to wash, dress or feed herself or walk unassisted. The husband hired several people in turn to care for her while he worked, but they also did the family cooking and light housework. The IRS conceded that the woman needed someone to stay with her and that services directly affecting her wellbeing were deductible as medical costs. But it disallowed 40% of the $2,785 deduction as simply payment for routine housework.

The Tax Court decided that the employes did spend "a majority of their time" performing medical services. It then raised the deductible portion to 75% from 60%.

(Frier v. Commissioner, T.C. Memo. 1971-84.)
5/12/71

A new ruling slightly eases the burden for parents of a retarded child.

Upon advice by a physician, they put their mentally retarded son in a special school run by a religious order. The main reason was availability of resources there to alleviate his handicap. The school was licensed by the state, which also gave the parents financial help by paying part of the tuition, room and board.

The IRS ruling this week was favorable to the parents. It held that the payments from the state were a scholarship. Thus they weren't taken into account in figuring whether the parents had provided more than one-half their son's support and could claim him as an exemption. The IRS so ruled the part the parents paid was a deductible medical expense.

(Rev. Ruling 71-347.)
8/4/71

School costs as medical expenses are mainly a factual issue, the Tax Court says.

Under tax regulations, if a child goes to a special school principally to overcome physical or mental handicaps, the entire costs are deductible medical expenses. But if the school isn't "special," only outlays specifically for medical care are deductible.

One recent case involved an emotionally troubled girl sent to a school for children with "special learning disabilities." The staff was well-trained in psychology and kept up-to-date through workshops. Psychiatrists were on call as consultants. Classes were small, flexible and ungraded. Children were allowed to set their own pace, and their programs were individually tailored for them. The Tax Court said the school readily qualified as special.

(Greisdorf v. Commissioner, 54 T.C. No. 167.)
10/7/70

Homes for the aged: It's tough but not impossible to deduct their fees.

A circuit court recently affirmed, without opinion, a previous Tax Court decision on whether room and board at a home for the elderly was deductible as a medical expense. The Tax Court had conceded that such costs "at an institution other than a hospital might constitute medical care." It's "a factual question," the court said. It depends "not upon the nature of the institution but the condition of the person and the care he receives."

In one case, the court had allowed a deduction for an elderly person who was totally unable to care for himself and relied on professional nursing at the home. But in this most recent case, the court refused the deduction because no medical care was received. The taxpayer's father was in good health and clear of mind. It didn't matter that, according to one witness, the old man couldn't have lived alone "with dignity" because he couldn't feed or dress himself properly.

That's not enough, the court said. "The general happiness and dignity with which a person lives is not the criteria."

(Robinson v. Commissioner, U.S. Ct. of Appeals, 9th Cir., 1970, affirming 52 T.C. 520.)
3/25/70

If you drive to the doctor's or use your car in rendering a service to a charity, your out-of-pocket expenses are deductible medical expenses or charitable gifts. These can be itemized, but since 1964 the IRS has also allowed a flat rate, which in October 1970, it raised to six cents a mile. It has never pinpointed exactly what that six cents a mile was meant to cover, however. This week, it ruled that tolls and parking fees can be claimed on top of the flat mileage rate.

(Rev. Procedure 70-12.)
4/29/70

Food and lodging as a medical deduction is allowed by an appeals court.

Back in the Fifties, Congress became concerned about people deducting the cost of a Florida vacation as taken on doctor's orders. It tightened the tax law to rule out a medical deduction for meals and lodging while away from home for medical treatment. Recently, however, the Seventh Circuit appeals court reversed the Tax Court and refused to find an "absolute" bar against such a deduction.

The case involved a Milwaukee man who was stricken with appendicitis while in New York City. The hospital was crowded, and he had to give up his room before he was ready to travel. Thus his doctor had him stay a week at a nearby hotel. Under these circumstances, his $184 hotel bill was "a true medical cost," the court said.

(Kelly v. Commissioner, U.S. Ct. of Appeals, 7th Cir., 1971.)
3/31/71

Medical travel deduction allows non-transport costs, says a circuit court.

The court backed the Tax Court in allowing a Kentucky couple to deduct $162 spent on food and lodging while traveling to the Mayo Clinic for the wife's medical treatment. The higher court brushed aside an IRS objection that living costs while being treated at a medical center away from home aren't deductible. The IRS would have held the couple's deduction to the bare cost of transportation.

The circuit court demurred. Congress had written the restriction on living expenses into the law because too many people were having their doctors prescribe a stay in Florida for their health. But the lawmakers didn't disturb the traditional medical deduction for travel.

(Montgomery v. Commissioner, U.S. Ct. of Appeals, 6th Cir., 1970.)
6/24/70

Brain-damage therapy can be deductible, even though administered by a layman. In "patterning," brain-damaged children are helped through normal motions like crawling in hopes that undamaged portions of the brain will pick up the pattern and assume control of such motions. The therapy requires several people to help, and most parents rely on volunteers. But if someone is paid, the IRS says that is a deductible medical expense. "Medical care" depends on the services rendered, not on who renders them.

(Rev. Ruling 70-170.)
4/22/70

Doctor's orders: The Tax Court accepts driving as deductible medical therapy.

The courts have been dubious about recognizing activities such as golf or dancing lessons as medical expenses, even when prescribed by a physician. Such pursuits are personal expenses, the courts have held. But now the Tax Court has accepted ordinary driving costs as deductible in a case involving a woman whose face had been mutilated in an auto accident.

The woman's doctor insisted she drive, both to alleviate her fears after the accident and to avoid the stares on public transportation. Her husband therefore bought a new Chrysler, which she drove extensively, as well as to and from the doctor's office. The IRS would allow only the mileage to medical appointments as a deduction, but the Tax Court was willing to accept "all the driving (she) did directly to alleviate her mental condition."

The court drew the line there, however. It wouldn't allow a deduction for the cost of her car as well.

(Bordas v. Commissioner, T.C. Memo. 1970-97.)
3/13/70

Medical deductions for the cost of educating a mentally retarded child were expanded by a recent IRS ruling. It involved a boy who attended a regular school 25 miles from home because it had a special curriculum for the "educable mentally handicapped," while nearby schools did not. The IRS said the curriculum made the school the equivalent of a special school (where charges are routinely deductible), and its facilities were "a principal reason" for the child going there.

(Rev. Ruling 70-285.)
6/17/70

Medical deductions were broadened a bit by a recent IRS ruling to explicitly include some capital outlays. The ruling involved a man who suffered from arthritis and a severe heart condition. On advice from a doctor, he had a shower stall built on the first floor of his house. The IRS ruled the plumbing costs were deductible because their primary purpose was medical care.

(Rev. Ruling 70-395.)
8/12/70

A wheelchair patient bought a specially equipped automobile, at a $1,500 premium over the $4,500 price of a standard car. The special design included exit and entry ramps, a higher roof, special doors, and locks to hold wheelchairs in place. All this made the outlay deductible as a medical expense, the IRS ruled, but only the extra $1,500.

(Rev. Ruling 70-605.)
12/16/70

The Tax Court denied a Los Angeles doctor, suffering from emphysema, a medical deduction for the cost of travel to and from a golf course for play. His physician has recommended the exercise. Light exercise might be desirable, the court said, but he could walk without golfing and could swing a club without swinging it on a course. The court was unmoved by his plea that exercise within Los Angeles was impossible because of smog and pollutants.

(Altman v. Commissioner, 53 T.C. No. 47.)
1/21/70

Legal fees to have someone committed to a mental institution are deductible as medical expenses, the IRS rules. The IRS hadn't allowed such a deduction, but it recently reversed its position in line with a 1969 court decision. In that case, doctors had advised commitment of a woman with a history of violent behavior and alcoholism. The court found "a direct or proximate relationship" between the legal fees and medical treatment.

(Rev. Ruling 71-281.)
7/14/71

A live-in maid is a help, but hardly medicinal, a U.S. court of appeals recently ruled. The case involved a heart-attack patient who lived alone. His doctor advised hiring a housekeeper to take his household chores off his hands and also to summon help if he were stricken again. The patient claimed a medical deduction for her salary, but the court said no. Her job was just to call for help, not to give medical aid, and relieving him of his chores bore no "direct and proximate therapeutic relation" to his health, it said.

(Borgmann v. Commissioner, U.S. Ct. of Appeals, 9th Cir., 1971.)
3/17/71

A staff doctor at a Veterans Administration hospital enjoyed the normal "professional courtesy" under which doctors don't bill one another for services rendered. He couldn't reciprocate or refer patients, so he bought $120 in gift certificates and gave them to seven doctors. The Tax Court refused him a medical deduction, however. He wasn't expected to pay, it said, and the $120 was simply a tangible, but token, expression of appreciation.

(O'Hare v. Commissioner, 54 T.C. No. 84.)
5/6/70

Social Security taxes keep going up, and Prentice-Hall Inc. offers a tip on shaving the tax bite. If an employer pays his employes while they are out sick, he should do so under a definite sick-pay plan because such payments aren't subject to Social Security. As the taxable wage base goes up—pending legislation would make it the first $10,200 beginning in 1972—more workers will find their entire pay subject to tax. Thus a switch to sick pay from wages will yield a saving.

7/28/71

Finding Tax Shelter at Home

An office at home may be deducted more easily under a circuit court decision.

When an employe keeps an office at home, the IRS has restricted any deduction for its cost to someone whose employer required him to do so. Recently, however, the Second Circuit ruled in favor of a television time salesman for ABC who deducted part of his rent, cleaning expenses and electric bill. He used a small study every evening to plan his rounds and watch ads on ABC and competing networks.

The IRS denied the deduction because ABC didn't require the study. If the salesman wanted to work late, the IRS said, the ABC office was open and little more than 20 blocks away. But the circuit court said no law restricts a business expense to an outlay required by one's employer. It was enough for the expense to be "appropriate and helpful" in one's work. The salesman had to see as much TV as he could, the court said, and what better place than "in the isolation of his study den"?

The salesman originally deducted one-fourth the expenses of a four-room apartment. But a lower court cut the deduction to 20% because the study was so small.

(Newi v. Commissioner, U.S. Ct. of Appeals, 2nd Cir., 1970.)
11/11/70

Here's an instance of when an office at home is a deductible business expense.

The courts have allowed a deduction in less clear-cut circumstances, but a recent Tax Court decision was almost a textbook case. It involved an airline pilot, who used the office for outside business pursuits as well as for paper work relating to his job. These included an unsuccessful stint selling for a family firm, real estate interests, and union activities.

The pilot put aside a room for exclusive use as an office, and he furnished it appropriately. It contained all his records, and at times he used it for meetings with union members. The court ruled that all this clearly established a need for the office, and the pilot's $338 deduction for depreciation, utilities and insurance was reasonable.

(Bailey v. Commissioner, T.C. Memo. 1971-107.)
6/2/71

Mortgage 'points' may be deductible as interest, the IRS rules.

With mortgage money under feverish demand, many lenders are extracting from borrowers a special, one-time charge—or "points"—in addition to a stated annual interest. Often this form is chosen to skirt state ceilings on interest rates. A charge of three points (or $3 on each $100 of mortgage principal) boosts to 7.4% the actual interest rate on $10,000 borrowed for 20 years ostensibly at 7%.

Until recently, the tax treatment of points has been in doubt. Now the IRS has said that points may be deductible as interest. A key part of the ruling: "By whatever name called, (interest) must be compensation for the use or forbearance of money per se." If points represent payment to a lender for services, such as checking an applicant's credit, they won't be deductible interest, the ruling indicated.

(Rev. Ruling 69-188.)
4/30/69

Mortgage points can be fully deducted in the year they are paid, the IRS says.

Earlier this year, the Revenue Service ruled that points were deductible as interest when they were in fact a payment "solely for the use or forbearance of money" (and not for services, such as checking the borrower's credit). Points are usually paid as a lump sum, however, and the IRS left unclear whether that sum was immediately deductible or had to be pro-rated over the life of the mortgage.

Now, in an advisory ruling, the tax service has concluded that pro-rating isn't required. The ruling concerned a $1,200 "loan processing fee" paid on a $20,000 mortgage, in addition to annual interest of 8%. The points didn't have to be pro-rated, the IRS said, because deducting them in the year paid wouldn't cause "a material distortion" of income for that year.

(Rev. Ruling 69-582.)
12/3/69

Selling a house: Are the costs of holding it for later sale deductible?

The law gives a tax deduction for expenses connected with "property held for the production of income," and some taxpayers have claimed the deduction in selling their home. A recent Tax Court case involved a Pine Bluff, Ark., couple who moved out of a home that cost $71,000. They asked $70,000 for it—considerably more than its market value. It was finally sold 14 months later for $50,000.

The couple claimed it was held for income (a possibly higher price) and wanted to deduct $3,750 for expenses and depreciation while the house was vacant. The Tax Court disagreed. If a homeowner merely wanted to recoup his investment, it was "difficult" to consider the house held for income, it said. Putting it on the market immediately was also "strong evidence" the owner didn't intend to hold it. An owner would have to show he expected the house would become more valuable than it was when he moved out.

Half a dozen Tax Court judges concurred in the denial of the deduction. They felt, however, a taxpayer needn't prove he was out to make a profit over his cost.

(Newcombe v. Commissioner, 54 T.C. No. 123.)
6/24/70

A court rebuffs an effort to mix business with pleasure.

It's estimated that Americans are building second homes at better than 150,000 a year. But the Tax Court recently rejected one effort to ease the expense of a home-away-from-home. A couple owned a $75,000 "cottage" at Sea Island, Ga., which they used four months a year and offered for rent the other eight. Rents never matched cash expenses plus depreciation, however, and they tried to deduct the difference from taxable income. (They only included expenses for the eight months.)

The Tax Court refused the deduction. It said the couple failed to show any intent to make a profit, rather than simply defray expenses. It noted that over 12 years, actual rentals averaged one month a year. But the court ducked the tougher question of whether a property could be used for pleasure part of a year and genuinely run for profit during the remainder.

(Carkhuff v. Commissioner, T.C. Memo. 1969-66.)
4/23/69

Mobile homes grow in numbers and importance but pose a tax tangle.

Last year, more than a third of new single-family houses were mobile homes, many of them spacious and comfortable. Such homes are still taxed in a hodgepodge of ways. Many states still consider them vehicles and levy low license fees. Others tax them as personal property. Mobile-home owners pay some real estate tax indirectly in their space rent.

The mobile-home boom feeds a running dispute on whether such homes pay their "fair" share of local taxes. Some California counties have suspended the issuance of permits for new mobile home-parks. In San Francisco, excluding land taxes, a mobile home pays about one-fourth the taxes a conventional home of like value would pay over 10 years. But others say that mobile-home owners pay for more than their share of services, mainly because such families are likely to be childless. In Macomb County near Detroit, mobile homes have one school child per four families, compared with six per four families for all housing.

The Mobile Home Manufacturers Association claims a proposed park near St. Louis would produce \$537 in taxes per school-age child, compared with \$150 from conventional housing on the same land.

3/18/70

Oh give me a home: The IRS Commissioner's annual report shows how home ownership fits into the tax scheme of things. Itemized deductions for 1968 (the latest figure available) came to \$69.18 billion. Of that, \$19.2 billion, or 28%, was directly related to home ownership; \$9.38 billion for real estate taxes and \$9.82 billion for interest on home mortgages. By comparison, \$11.14 billion was deducted for charitable gifts and \$8.49 billion for medical or dental expenses.

5/12/71

A Few Points on Moving

When IBM covers an employe's "loss" on his home, that's income, a court rules.

The initials IBM stand for "I've been moved," some long-time employes of International Business Machines Corp. say ruefully. With so many transfers, the giant company is relatively thorough in cushioning the financial burden of moving. Under its "home guarantee policy," the company paid an employe the $2,000 difference between the $58,000 appraised value of his home and the $56,000 he sold it for.

The taxpayer argued that the $2,000 was simply part of the sales proceeds, and as his new house cost much more than the old, there was no gain to tax. This argument impressed neither the IRS nor the Tax Court. Recently a circuit court also ruled the sum was ordinary income for the taxpayer.

The new Tax Reform Act counts reimbursed moving costs as income, but it then allows most taxpayers to deduct certain costs in selling their house and buying a new one. But the deductible costs don't include any such paper "loss" on a home.

(Lull v. Commissioner, U.S. Ct. of Appeals, 9th Cir., 1970.)
12/9/70

The IRS denies a deduction for the cost of moving new furniture.

Normally, a taxpayer who moves to a new job site is entitled to deduct the cost of moving his furniture (and certain other outlays). Last week, however, the IRS denied a deduction to a taxpayer who moved from England to Colorado but bought new furniture in Massachusetts en route. The deduction doesn't apply to new furniture, the IRS said.

The law doesn't require that furniture come directly from the old residence to the new. It could come out of storage, the IRS said, as long as it had been used before. The cost of moving used household goods from a place other than the former residence is deductible to the extent it doesn't exceed what it would have cost for a move from the former residence.

The IRS ruling doesn't specify how long it takes "new" furniture to become "used." According to Tax Coordinator, an advisory service, elsewhere in the tax law where use is required for a reduction, even one day is technically sufficient.

(Rev. Ruling 70-625.)
12/23/70

Moving expenses, under the Tax Reform Act, must be included in gross income if they are reimbursed or paid (directly or indirectly) by one's employer. Normally the employe can offset that income by also deducting the expenses, provided they meet certain tests. Last week the IRS recognized this wash-out effect. It ruled that the employer's payment isn't subject to withholding "if it is reasonable to believe at the time of payment that a corresponding deduction is allowable."

(Rev. Ruling 70-482.)
9/23/70

Moving season: Of the 14.5 million working people who moved last year, about one million were eligible for tax deductions for moving expenses, the IRS says. (If an employer reimburses the expenses, such payments count as income, which is then offset with appropriate deductions.) Starting this year, employers must give their employes a new IRS form detailing moving expenses paid on their behalf. The new Form 4782 will be available in mid-August, the IRS says.

(IRS News Release IR-1154, 1971.)
7/28/71

Citizen soldier: A serviceman moved his family overseas to his new post, even though it was against the rules at his new station for his family to come along. The IRS ruled that as long as the soldier met normal tax law rules about moving expenses in connection with a new place of work, he was entitled to deduct his family's moving costs. His violation of the Army's housing preferences didn't cut any ice.

(Rev. Ruling 70-520.)
10/21/70

Moving expenses, when job-related, are normally deductible, and that includes travel by car from the old residence to the new one. In such instances, taxpayers may deduct a flat six cents a mile in lieu of keeping detailed travel expense records, the IRS recently ruled. Parking and tolls are deducted separately.

(Rev. Procedure 71-2.)
1/27/71

Three years too soon: In denying a California couple's deduction of certain moving expenses in 1967, the Tax Court noted that most costs of their move would have been deductible beginning this year under the 1969 reform act. Most transferred employes and self-employed persons moving to new job locations can now deduct basic expenses of selling a house and buying a new one, settling an unexpired lease, and living up to 30 days while house-hunting at a new location.

(Kay v. Commissioner, T.C. Memo. 1970-202.)
7/22/70

Tax Aspects of Giving

Libraries lament that a tax change has dried up gifts of personal papers.

John Updike isn't giving his manuscripts to Harvard anymore, and Harvard blames the Tax Reform Act. Archibald MacLeish has shifted from giving his papers to the Library of Congress to just leaving them on deposit. Poet Karl Shapiro has similarly stopped donating his manuscripts to the Library of Congress, and cartoonist Bill Mauldin is also upset. In fact, last year the Library received "virtually no gifts" of works created by the donor, a spokesman says.

The problem, library officials say, is that formerly an author could donate his papers and claim a healthy charitable deduction for their fair market value. The Tax Reform Act, however, limits a donor's deduction to what a gift manuscript cost him—in the case of an author, little more than paper and ink. The result, libraries across the country claim, has brought gifts of musical scores, manuscripts, personal papers or documents to a halt.

Sen. Frank Church has introduced legislation that would restore an author-donor's tax break to about half its former level. The Church bill "isn't as good as we'd like, but it's so much better than what we have now," one library spokesman says.

3/24/71

Give until it hurts: Tax treatment eases the pain of large gifts, fund-raisers say.

Professional fund-raisers argue that tougher tax treatment of large charitable gifts may cripple university and hospital campaigns to raise capital funds.

"Eighty-five per cent of your money comes from 15% of your donors," says A. C. Barnett of Tamblyn & Brown Inc. Very large gifts are "totally and completely all-important," declares Robert L. Conway of John Price Jones Co. He says a $20 million campaign typically must garner at least one $5 million gift, two of $2 million and three of $1 million. A recent survey found some 112 schools seeking $4 billion in capital funds.

Fund-raisers contend that tax angles rarely move people to give. "I've never had anyone say, 'What the hell, it won't cost me much. Who can I give it to?'" claims Austin V. McClain of Marts & Lundy Inc. Attorney Conrad Teitell agrees—but "once you do believe in Olde Ivy, taxes become very important." Barnett recalls one would-be donor of $50,000 who was shown how to raise his to $500,000 by giving away appreciated land. "It cost him practically nothing," Barnett says.

Philanthropist Louis Schweitzer says he gives away as much as tax law permits him to deduct. "There's no question" the law encourages giving, he says.

4/16/69

Giving to charity climbs steadily with income, itemized returns for 1968 show.

The higher a person's income, the larger his charitable contributions usually are. That expectation is borne out by IRS statistics summarized by the American Association of Fund-Raising Counsel. Taxpayers with adjusted gross income of $5,000-to-$10,000 averaged $221 in deductible gifts. In the $10,000-to-$15,000 range, the figure was $312; and for $15,000-to-$20,000, the deduction rose to $434. At the $20,000-to-$25,000 level, the average gifts skipped to $586, and then to $714 for the $25,000-to-$30,000 bracket.

Normally, richer people give away a greater proportion of their income, too, but the IRS figures show an anomaly. Givers in the modest $5,000-to-$10,000 category gave a larger portion of their income to charity (2.9%) than all others except those who earned $50,000 or more. At that height, the average was 3.4% or better.

10/29/70

A minister's word prevails in Tax Court over IRS legal objections.

In many Tax Court cases, taxpayers represent themselves and at times rely on simple fairness, unadorned by legal niceties. Over the years, the court has shown itself remarkably open to their pleas. One recent case concerned a New Mexico man, a minister in the Word of Life Church, whose flock had dwindled to his family and four or five friends. The minister said he tithed scrupulously, handled the church's money and paid its bills. But he kept no records at all.

The IRS disallowed his $727 contributions deduction as unsubstantiated. Further, it argued, the church lacked a charter, hadn't shown it merited an exemption, and amounted to the parson's personal venture. But the court accepted testimony that there really was an active group, albeit a small one, that pursued a religious purpose. It also believed the minister made the donations he claimed.

(Blake v. Commissioner, T.C. Memo. 1970-117.)
5/27/70

Some skiers find a tax deduction to ease their runs down the slopes.

If a taxpayer works for a charitable cause, his out-of-pocket outlays are normally deductible. This winter, many of the 22,000 members of the National Ski Patrol System Inc. are taking advantage of the provision to defray the hefty costs of the sport. The patrol volunteers serve as safety monitors and offer first aid at about 750 ski areas, mostly in the U.S.

Normally the patrolmen's expense for food, lodging

and transportation qualify. One New Yorker commutes weekends to Vermont by small plane and deducts part of the plane's upkeep. Special ski gear used for patrol duties can usually be claimed. "It's something you do, but you do it with discretion," says a Wall Street broker and patrol skier. Linda Curtis of New York City, a patrol member for four years, says the deduction is "obviously a side benefit" but a substantial one.

Patrol members must meet tough standards, prowl long hours over ski runs, and perform many nonskiing duties. "Anyone who does it for the tax break has got to be out of his mind," says Edward L. Ericson of National Ski Patrol.

1/28/70

Legal fees a donor paid to defend a park from highways are ruled deductible.

In 1924, the late Anne Archbold gave the U.S. land that became part of Glover-Archbold Park in the District of Columbia. Three decades later, a highway was proposed that would have destroyed half the park. Mrs. Archbold hired a law firm to resist the plan, and it was shelved. Similar encroachments were threatened in the early 1960s, and Mrs. Archbold paid a total of $30,000 in legal fees. Along the way, Congress passed a five-year freeze on highways through the park.

The Court of Claims recently ruled that Mrs. Archbold was entitled to deduct her legal fees as a gift "for the use of" the U.S. This applied even though "elements" of the government (the Interior Department for one) were the target of her suits. That made the case "slightly thorny," the court said, but Congress had accepted the original gift, and its voice was crucial in approving or disapproving Mrs. Archbold's later efforts. The court interpreted the freeze on construction as conveying congressional approval.

That didn't mean the public-at-large could get a

similar deduction. A donor "enjoys a continuing relationship to his gift which others don't have," the court said.

(Archbold v. U.S., U.S. Ct. of Claims, 1971)
7/28/71

The IRS allows a deduction for expenses in a project to help unwed mothers.

Normally the IRS won't allow a deduction for contributions made directly to an individual, no matter how worthy. Similarly, gifts to a charity aren't deductible if they are earmarked for a particular person. Recently, however, the IRS found its way to allow such outlays by one family, even though they were spent to help a particular girl.

Under the program, a pregnant woman was taken into the home of the volunteer family, which was expected to treat her as a member of the household. The family was to provide proper diet and clothing and a small weekly allowance. The woman, in turn, was expected to lend a hand with household chores, but she wasn't to be considered an employe. In this context, the IRS ruled the family was helping the sponsoring charity carry out its program, and its expenses were contributions.

But the IRS ruled out a deduction for expenses the family would have incurred anyway, such as rent and utilities.

(Rev. Ruling 69-473.)
9/17/69

A "Big Brother" may deduct some of what he spends on his young charge.

Donations to individuals, no matter how worthy, aren't deductible as charitable gifts. Nor are such donations deductible even when made through charities if the donor picks the recipient. Recently the IRS ruled, however, that out-of-pocket expenses by a "big brother" volunteer qualified as deductible. The volunteer group was formed to provide guidance to potentially delinquent boys "who lacked the influence of mature and responsible men."

The IRS said such volunteers often take boys places and incur costs for meals and admissions. No volunteer selects the boy he works with, the IRS said. Thus it concluded that reasonable, unreimbursed outlays for "swimming, attending movies, going out to dinner, fishing and the like" are deductible. But the service permits no deduction for the volunteer's own expenses, because he benefits in return (seeing a movie, for example).

Tax Coordinator, a tax reporting service, questioned this last qualification. "If a taxpayer entertains customers," it said, "he (may) deduct his share of the entertainment bill along with his customers."

(Rev. Ruling 70-519.)
10/21/70

An adoption fee isn't a gift, even though based on income, the Tax Court rules.

In recent years, most adoption agencies have moved from asking adoptive parents for a donation to charging a fee for professional services rendered. The fees are nevertheless commonly based on income and ability to pay. In one typical case, the Talbot Perkins Adoption Service in New York charged $1,750—that is, 10% of the adoptive father's income.

The adoptive parents sought to deduct the payment as a charitable gift. They noted that it was tied to income, rather than to services rendered, and in addition it wasn't mandatory—it was waived if a couple couldn't afford it. But the Tax Court nevertheless found it a fee for "a significant and direct benefit to them." If a great discrepancy existed between the fee and what the services were worth, the payment could be part fee and part gift, the court said. But no discrepancy was shown.

(Murphy v. Commissioner, 54 T.C. No. 22.)
2/25/70

She provided a place for homeless teen-agers, but the refuge wasn't deductible.

As new needs emerge, charitable giving changes its face, but not all giving is tax-sheltered. In California, a social worker provided food and shelter for teen-agers who had been turned out by their parents or left home. She said her religious beliefs wouldn't allow her "to turn a youngster into the street and not feed him," so the stray teen-agers were welcome to stay with her and her family. The young people drifted in and out; over a year, she spent $2,400 on their support.

The California woman sought to deduct those expenses on her tax return, but the Tax Court said no. Tax law doesn't permit a deduction for contributions to individuals, no matter how worthy. The court managed to turn up a degree of tax relief, however. It noted that one teen-ager had lived with her family the entire year. She could claim him as her dependent.

Actually the boy had been gone two months "when he was really out of his head and was in the streets." But the court ruled that was an absence "by reason of illness," which doesn't count as breaching the entire-year rule.

(Dollar v. Commissioner, T.C. Memo. 1971-177.)
8/4/71

Avery Brundage, president of the International Olympic Committee, bested the IRS in a recent tax tangle. It concerned the gift in 1963 of his renowned Asian art collection to San Francisco for the de Young Memorial Museum. A taxpayer could then deduct up to 30% of his income as a gift to "educational organizations" (currently, it's 50%), but only 20% to ordinary charities. The IRS argued the museum wasn't an educational organization, but Brundage convinced the Tax Court it was.

(Brundage v. Commissioner, 54 T.C. No. 139.)
7/15/70

Gosh, Sarge, you never appreciated me: A U.S. district court jury in Connecticut concluded that 1,055 original Beetle Bailey cartoons were worth $28,000 when they were donated to Syracuse University. The decision means that Mort Walker, who draws the woeful soldier, will be able to claim a charitable contribution of that amount for income tax purposes.

(Walker v. U.S.A., U.S. Dist. Ct., Dist. Conn. 1969.)
7/2/69

By the book: James L. Robertson, Federal Reserve Board vice chairman, wanted to give Uncle Sam the royalties from his book "What Generation Gap???" but "absolutely amazing" Treasury red tape deterred him, he says. To keep the donated proceeds from being taxed as income would have required: A ruling from the Internal Revenue Commissioner, assignment of copyright to the Treasury and at least three other legal steps that "just weren't worth my time," Mr. Robertson says. A college will get the royalties.

2/4/70

The septic tanks in a low-lying Houston suburb never worked, so about 40 homeowners chipped in $1,560 each to put in a water and sewage system. They turned the system over to their village, which had agreed to maintain it. One homeowner sought to deduct the $1,560 as a charitable gift, but the IRS balked. So did the Tax Court, even though the man said he expected nothing in return for his outlay. Maintenance by the village was "an anticipated benefit of an economic nature," the court said.

(Wolfe v. Commissioner, 54 T.C. No. 170.)
8/16/70

No gift: The Tax Court recently held that C. F. Mueller Co., a pasta maker owned by a voting trust for the benefit of New York University School of Law, couldn't deduct $445,000 in "contributions" to the Law Center Foundation at NYU. The sum would have to come out of after-tax earnings, the court said. Otherwise, the arrangement would get around a law that if a tax-exempt group owns an ordinary business, it must pay taxes on what it earns.

(C.F. Mueller Co. v. Commissioner, 55 T.C. No. 28.)
11/18/70

Some gift: The Tax Court denied an Oregon man a $2,757 charitable deduction for giving 700 pounds of suppositories to an old people's home. They had been left in his basement by the prior occupant, a drug salesman, and they ended up in the county dump.

(Goodman v. Commissioner, T.C. Memo. 1970-122.)
5/27/70

A big game hunter brought down a clean kill in darkest Texas. A U.S. district court jury decided he could deduct as a charitable gift the cost of a safari trip to Kenya. It accepted his claim that the hunt was arranged to bag specimens for an American museum. The court ordered a $6,700 tax refund.

(Jersis v. U.S.A., U.S. Dist. Ct., West Dist. Texas, 1968.)
4/16/69

A Bas Mitzvah wasn't deductible, the Tax Court told a California couple. The court disallowed a deduction of $567 the couple paid their temple for their daughter's event. "This is not a charitable contribution, just as the cost of a wedding is not a charitable contribution," the court said. "Although each occasion has religious significance, it is primarily a social event."

(Feistman v. Commissioner, T.C. Memo. 1971-137.)
6/30/71

Larger deductions for charitable donations may be sustained if you take it to court. One taxpayer recently claimed $600 in church contributions, but the IRS chopped that to a nominal $52 for lack of proof. The Tax Court, however, found reasonable his testimony that he went to church every Sunday and put at least $10 in the plate each time. The court restored $540 of the $600.

(Grinis v. Commissioner, T.C. Memo. 1970-94.)
5/13/70

A taxpayer's blood ought to qualify for a deduction, some Congressmen say. About two dozen lawmakers are backing a bill introduced by Rep. Edward I. Koch (D., N.Y.) to grant a $25 deduction for each pint of blood (up to five annually) donated to the Red Cross or other nonprofit blood-collecting units. Existing tax law considers giving blood rendering a service, and donated services aren't deductible.

7/21/71

Playboy philanthropy: Cornell University library has put out an appeal for early issues of Playboy and says that such donations would be tax-deductible. "Early issues are almost unattainable on the scholarly book market, especially in complete state, with the centerfold that researchers are known to find of particular interest," the library bulletin deadpans. Despite the tax break, Cornell has yet to move any bibliophiles to part with their magazines, a university spokesman says.

10/15/69

A private school levied a certain tuition fee but also required each pupil's family to make a "donation" of twice that amount. The IRS recently refused to grant a tax deduction to cushion the burden, however. A donation, it said, is "a voluntary transfer" made with donative intent and not for consideration. In this case, there was consideration—enrollment in the school—and the "donation" wasn't deductible as a charitable contribution, the IRS said.

(Rev. Ruling 71-112.)
3/10/71

Cutting Your Losses

Ice storm losses are deductible, but more storms may brew over how much.

The IRS should absorb some of the losses from the ice storm last week that downed trees and glazed much of the Northeast. Storm damage, if uninsured, is deductible as a casualty loss, to the extent it exceeds $100. The rub comes, however, in establishing the dollar amount. Contrary to some expectations, the loss isn't measured by what it costs to repair or replace the property. The loss is the difference in property's value before the storm and after.

Ornamental trees and shrubbery are "an integral part of the real property," the IRS has said in a similar context. Thus the loss is the "actual decrease in the value of the property as a whole." Replacement costs don't decide the issue, but they are acceptable "as evidence of decrease in value." In one case where expensive boxwoods were damaged the court gave their replacement cost "some secondary weight," but it determined the loss by the overall-value rule.

Courts have accepted the cost of cleaning up storm debris as a storm loss and also the cost of removing a limb from a storm-damaged tree.

12/16/70

Another home in California slides in value without incurring a casualty loss.

The Tax Court recently decided another case growing out of the 1965 slides in Pacific Palisades, when a great many lovely homes overlooking the Pacific almost ended up in it. The controversial tax point is that while most homes suffered minor physical damage or none, property values tumbled in the entire area. In this case, the home was worth $65,000 before the slide, but only $42,000 afterwards. The owners simply moved out, sacrificing their $21,094 equity in the property.

The taxpayers claimed a $21,094 casualty loss, but the Tax Court agreed with the IRS in denying the claim. The court found the loss in value was attributable mainly to "general buyer resistance" and "only to a minor degree" to post-slide cracks that appeared in the property. Physical damage or destruction is "an inherent prerequisite" of a casualty loss, it said. Thus when the owners moved out in early 1966, they incurred a nondeductible personal loss, not a casualty loss, because they chose to dispose of the home while its value was down.

The court chopped their casualty loss to $1,000, which it concluded was the actual damage the slide inflicted.

(Kamanski v. Commissioner, T.C. Memo. 1970-352.)
1/20/71

A Maryland couple beats the IRS in the elusive task of calculating a loss.

In tax law, the measure of a casualty loss is simply the difference in the fair market value of the property immediately before and immediately after the casualty. But how do you set the fair market value of goods that were never meant to be sold? The couple were burned out of their home, and the entire contents of the house destroyed. They hired an adjuster, who said the goods had been worth $42,521: their $55,568 cost, less $13,047 in depreciation.

By contrast, the IRS claimed their things had been worth a mere $15,304, but the Tax Court threw that figure out. The IRS had tried to prove what the goods would have fetched "if hawked off by a secondhand dealer or at a forced sale." That wouldn't do, the court said, because it wasn't a reasonable measure of the "actual value" to the couple. The method the taxpayers relied on—original cost less 20% or 25% for depreciation—struck the court as "fair and reasonable."

For one thing, the court said, insurance companies also used the couple's method. And they obviously had no interest in inflating loss figures.

(Cornelius v. Commissioner, 56 T.C. No. 77.)
8/19/71

An ice fisherman's car took an unexpected swim, but the IRS accepted the plunge as a casualty loss and allowed a tax deduction. The car, which was uninsured, was parked on an ice-covered lake, where the owner was fishing. The ice suddenly gave way, and the car sank to the bottom, a total loss.

(Rev. Ruling 69-88.)
3/12/69

A casualty loss, to be deductible, must be due to a sudden, unexpected or unusual cause. Slow death doesn't qualify, the Tax Court recently ruled. A couple paid a premium price for a wooded lot, graced by beeches and maples. A month later, the lot was graded improperly, and fill dirt blocked aeration of the trees' roots. The inept grading doomed the trees, but the court said their death was from "progressive deterioration," a gradual suffocation over 16 months.

(Miller v. Commissioner, T.C. Memo. 1970-167.)
7/8/70

Earthquake damage in Los Angeles County can be claimed as a disaster loss on 1970 returns even though the quake occurred in early 1971. This quick-relief procedure is allowed whenever the President declares a disaster area, and the disaster happens before the due date for prior year returns. Thus far only Los Angeles County has been named, but other counties are under consideration, officials say.

(IRS Announcement 71-18.)
3/17/71

Some home mishaps are deductible, the IRS agrees. When a husband accidentally slammed a car door on his wife's hand, her 1.38 carat diamond popped from its setting, never to be seen again. At tax time, the couple claimed a $1,200 casualty loss, but the IRS demurred. It considered their misfortune an ordinary household mishap, like a boy tearing his new pants. But the Tax Court judged it a true casualty loss, caused by a sudden, unexpected, violent event. The IRS recently acquiesced in the ruling.

(White v. Commissioner, 48 T.C. No. 42.)
6/11/69

Shock of recognition: A Virginia couple discovered $2,729 in termite damage, even though exterminators had found "no visible evidence" of termites when the couple bought their house about four months before. The Tax Court wouldn't allow a casualty loss, however. A "casualty" must be sudden, it said, and the termites had been chewing away for years. (Previous owners had known this.) The court sympathized with the couple's "catastrophic shock," but their "sudden realization" doesn't make the damage sudden.

(Sahkul v. Commissioner, T.C. Memo. 1970-60.)
3/25/70

Totaled: A Maryland couple gave their 20-year-old son $1,000 to buy a car. He bought a used Austin-Healey roadster, which was registered in his name. Even before he acquired collision coverage, one of his friends smashed up the car. At tax time, the parents claimed a casualty loss, but the Tax Court turned them down. They had given the $1,000 to their son, and the casualty loss was his.

(Oman v. Commissioner, T.C. Memo. 1971-183.)
8/4/71

In a burglary it can be tough to prove the value of items stolen from you, or that you ever owned them at all. In one recent case, a Brooklyn man claimed he lost $434 in cash, a TV set, and two diamond rings, but the IRS recognized no theft loss whatsoever. He appealed to the Tax Court, which proved less sticky. He argued his own case, and the Tax Court believed him. It cut the estimated loss to $1,209 from $1,489, however.

(Farrior v. Commissioner, T.C. Memo. 1970-312.)
11/25/70

Communist Rumania confiscated an art collection after the war, but the owner couldn't claim a theft deduction for the loss, a court of appeals recently ruled. Taking private property "under color of governmental action" isn't theft. The widow of the last pre-war U.S. Minister to Rumania lodged the claim.

(Farcasanu v. Commissioner, U.S. Ct. of Appeals, D.C. Cir., 1970.)
9/2/70

Gem lode: The Tax Court accepted a taxpayer's unlikely and unsupported claim that he had lost some diamonds when his garage burned down. It seems he hid them there to keep them out of his estranged wife's hands.

(Williams v. Commissioner, T.C. Memo. 1970-143.)
6/17/70

Theft loss claims again fare better in Tax Court than with the IRS. The law allows a casualty deduction for the portion of theft losses that exceeds $100, but the

IRS can be very sticky about proof that the theft occurred. In one recent case, the IRS entirely disallowed a taxpayer's $2,285 claim for a coin collection, some cash stashed away, a TV set and other personal goods. The Tax Court allowed the deduction but it cut the amount in half.

(Pharr v. Commissioner, T.C. Memo. 1971-28.)
3/3/71

Deducting Travel and Schooling

Summer travel: The Tax Court draws some lines on when the costs are deductible.

A New York City man and wife, both high school teachers, took a charter flight to Europe, rented a car and toured France. The IRS claimed their expenses weren't deductible because the trip wasn't "primarily undertaken" to maintain or improve job skills. But the court said it was enough that "the major portion" of the travel was directly related to such skills. On this basis, it ruled the wife's expenses were deductible, but her husband's weren't.

The husband taught Latin, and the court found "only a tenuous relationship" between visiting two Roman sites in France and his work. His wife, however, taught world civilization, and their itinerary clearly centered on places of importance in her instruction. It was "significant," the court said, that the couple shunned a group tour for the flexibility of going their own way. The trip helped the wife give a more "stimulating presentation" of her course.

The entire car rental and gasoline costs were deductible (because the wife wouldn't have paid less had she traveled alone) but only her share of other outlays.

(Marlin v. Commissioner, 54 T.C. No. 49.)
4/1/70

A young lawyer won his claim to deduct the cost of getting a master's degree.

It isn't easy to justify a deduction for graduate

study, but he managed. The law allows a deduction for education undertaken to maintain or improve skills required in a taxpayer's trade or business. There's no deduction, however, for schooling to meet the minimum education required to enter the field, or for schooling that's part of a program that leads to qualifying for a new field.

A recent case involved a young man who passed the Georgia bar in his third year of law school. The following summer, he worked for an Atlanta firm, then entered a master's program at Harvard Law. He tried to deduct all the education expenses he incurred after passing the bar, but the Tax Court drew a line. His final two quarters at law school weren't deductible because they were part of the program qualifying him to practice law. But the court allowed a deduction for his work at Harvard, mainly because the IRS conceded that if he had been a lawyer before he entered Harvard, his expenses would be deductible.

The court said he had clearly worked as a lawyer for the Atlanta firm. It also implied the IRS conceded too much in limiting its case to that point.

(Ruehmann v. Commissioner, T.C. Memo. 1971-157.)
7/14/71

School's out: It's still tough to justify education costs as business expenses.

An IRS agent recently sought to deduct the cost of graduate courses at a business school. The Tax Court found, however, that the schooling wasn't intended to maintain or improve skills required in his present job, but to qualify him for a better post. That's not deductible, it said. In another case, a high school teacher and his wife, a guidance counselor, toured the world for five months on sabbatical leave at half-pay. But they failed to persuade the court the trip was taken to maintain or improve their teaching skills. The tour was merely of general cultural value, the court said.

(Menas v. Commissioner, T.C. Memo. 1969-114.)

Another taxpayer's petition was denied because his schooling was too closely related to his work. An IBM engineer claimed the salary IBM paid him while it sent him to graduate school was a non-taxable fellowship. But the court noted that IBM passed on his choice of school and his research topic.

"Participants in the program were obviously viewed by IBM as undertaking regular job assignments," it said.

6/18/69

A teaching assistant flunks the Tax Court's tests for a business deduction.

As fellowship money becomes scarcer, more graduate students rely on jobs as teaching assistants. Recently the Tax Court decided a test case on whether a teaching assistant could deduct tuition and fees as a business expense. The taxpayer, an assistant in the zoology department at the University of Minnesota, contended that the university required him to be enrolled to retain his job. Further, he argued, he had already satisfied the minimum education to obtain the job (a bachelor's degree).

The Tax Court ruled against him. For one thing, it said, he had to be a student to obtain—not retain—his job. The post was temporary, and having it one year didn't mean he would have it again the next. (Educational expenses to obtain a position aren't deductible.) Beyond that, the court said, his real goal was to become a college professor, and he was still working on the Ph.D. required for that.

Two concurring judges would have given the claim

even shorter shrift. "Petitioner worked because he studied," they said. "He did not study because he worked."

(Jungreis v. Commissioner, 55 T.C. No. 58.)
1/6/71

Study abroad proved deductible in part for a Brooklyn, N.Y., junior high school teacher. The Tax Court allowed her to deduct $1,582 for a five-week summer course at Sophia University in Tokyo. The course was directly relevant to her teaching. The court, however, denied a $406 deduction for her return via South Asia, the Middle East and Rome. That was mainly for pleasure, the court decided.

(Weiman v. Commissioner, T.C. Memo. 1971-92.)
5/5/71

Aphrodite's trip doesn't stimulate the Tax Court. With her employer's approval, Aphrodite Thanos, a high school librarian, substituted a trip to Europe for required attendance at summer school. She visited historical sites, collected books, pamphlets and pictures for library use, and deducted the cost of the trip as an educational expense. The Tax Court upheld the IRS disallowance of the deduction. The court ruled the trip might have made the librarian generally more capable but didn't directly maintain or improve her prime skills as the deduction rules required.

(Thanos v. Commissioner, T.C. Memo. 1970-193.)
7/22/70

School expenses to qualify a taxpayer for a new trade aren't deductible, but one fellow who went to television-repair school tried a new twist. He sought to deduct what the final six months of a two-year program cost him. That portion dealt with color TV and solid-state circuitry, he said, and his earlier lessons had already qualified him to fix black-and-white sets. Thus the final six months were to improve existing job skills, he claimed, not to enter a new trade. The Tax Court found the two portions inseparable and entirely nondeductible.

(Betz v. Commissioner, T.C. Memo. 1971-29.)
2/17/71

Shot down: A reserve officer in the Air Force sought to deduct the cost of completing his college degree, but the Tax Court refused. The officer argued that without a degree, he couldn't get a regular commission; and without that, he would have to retire after 20 years. The court decided he was trying to better his status, rather than maintain it, and while the Air Force encouraged a college education, it didn't expressly require it.

(Kinch v. Commissioner, T.C. Memo. 1971-117.)
6/7/71

Grossinger's, the Catskills resort, had a fellow to entertain guests with "the art and science of hypnosis." He lacked formal training, so the management, fearful of being sued, ordered him to get some qualifications. That was in 1957. By 1966, he was a Ph.D. in psychology and almost a licensed psychologist. He tried to deduct his schooling, but the Tax Court wasn't entranced. His education "far exceeded" what Grossinger's, his employer, required, it said.

(Fleischer v. Commissioner, T.C. Memo. 1971-163.)
7/21/71

Working Away From Home

The overnight rule for deducting meal costs withstands a tough practical test.

Under its "overnight" rule, the IRS allows a business traveler to deduct the cost of meals only if his trip requires a stop for sleep or rest. The Supreme Court upheld the rule in 1969. The test seems even firmer now, following another decision in the Court of Appeals for the First Circuit. That case was interesting because it was brought by a taxpayer who put in extremely strenuous one-day travel but still failed to win a deduction.

The taxpayer, Frederick J. Barry, a consulting engineer, routinely left his home by 6:30 a.m. for business trips and didn't return until 10:30 p.m. or midnight. He ate all his meals on the road, and—for safety's sake, he said—normally pulled over for a refreshing nap before completing the drive home. But the circuit court upheld the Tax Court in deciding that a catnap wasn't what was meant by "sleep or rest." That required a stop long enough to entail "a significant increase in expenses."

The court didn't want to breach the clearcut overnight rule. "The tax involved is too small to warrant case by case haggling," it said.

(Barry v. Commissioner, U.S. Ct. of Appeals, 1st Cir., 1970.)
1/20/71

How long is "temporary"? The Tax Court upholds a taxpayer but ducks an answer.

If a person works away from his home temporarily, his traveling and living costs are deductible. The catch, however, is that if the new employment becomes more than temporary, the taxpayer's "tax home" is presumed to have moved to the new site, and living expenses become nondeductible personal outlays again. It isn't necessary for the new job to become permanent—indefinite is enough.

Recently the Tax Court had to decide whether a steam fitter's stint had slipped from temporary to indefinite. When construction work dried up in his home city, his union found him work elsewhere. In April 1967, he went to work on a nuclear power plant. He thought the job might last six months, but in fact it ran on for 31 months. On his 1967 return, the IRS disallowed his deduction of $2,562 in living and traveling expenses, but the Tax Court ruled for him. It noted that "complication after complication" had prolonged the thorny job.

The court didn't say how long "temporary" could be. It simply said that the job hadn't become indefinite by the end of 1967, the tax year involved in the litigation.

(Brown v. Commissioner, T.C. Memo. 1971-7.)
1/20/71

Home is where you hang your hat? The Tax Court tries to find a consistent rule.

The court returned to a perennial issue last week and tried to clarify it. The issue is deciding when a taxpayer is temporarily away from home on business and thus entitled to deduct his living costs. The case involved a teacher who lived in Knoxville, Tenn., but couldn't find a job there. He taught a year in Georgia and then a semester in North Carolina, while his family remained in Tennessee.

The Tax Court decided the two stints weren't what the law meant by being away temporarily. Ultimately, it said, the issue turns on whether under all the circumstances, the taxpayer could reasonably be expected to move his residence to near his work. The court decided the teacher had no business ties to Knoxville. Considering how bleak the job prospects were there, he might well be expected to move his family to greener pastures. Thus living in Knoxville but working elsewhere was a personal choice, it said.

It wasn't the same, the court said, as a taxpayer whose employer sent him elsewhere temporarily, or whose work forced him to take jobs "of necessarily brief duration in disparate localities."

(Tucker v. Commissioner, 55 T.C. No. 82.)
3/3/71

The IRS eases its posture on when a taxpayer is away from home.

The taxpayer may deduct travel and living expenses while "away from home" on business, but that apparently simple phrase has spawned many disputes. The IRS contends that a taxpayer's "tax home" is his regular place of work. (If he chooses to live elsewhere, that's a nondeductible commute.) In some cases, however, the IRS argued that a taxpayer had no tax home at all because he worked at several sites rather than one. Thus he couldn't deduct expenses for being away.

Last week, the IRS backed down a bit by ruling that someone who lacks a "principal place of employment" may nevertheless have a tax home. The ruling concerned a construction worker who worked at sites over a 12-state area. Considering "all the facts and circumstances," the IRS said, the man's tax home was his residence, where his family lived and where he lived when he wasn't traveling.

The ruling carefully noted that his trips were long enough to require his stopping for "substantial sleep or rest." Normally, one isn't considered away from home on business unless the trip is at least overnight.

(Rev. Ruling 71-247.)
6/16/71

Does your "home" move around? A Second Circuit decision is raising doubts.

A taxpayer's expenses while "away from home" on business are deductible, but the matter isn't simple. The IRS argues that when a taxpayer takes a job at a new location for an indefinite period, the new job site becomes his fictional "tax home." He isn't "away from home," even though his residence hasn't changed. On this theory, a U.S. district court denied a deduction to Ethel Merman, the Broadway star. She claimed she was away from her Colorado home while playing in "Gypsy," a two-year Broadway run.

The Second Circuit appeals court recently told the district court to look again and ignore the "tax home" hocus-pocus. What mattered was whether Miss Merman's expenses were compelled by her business affairs. The key question, the higher court said, was whether her New York stint was indefinite enough that "a reasonable person in her position would pull up stakes and make her permanent residence in New York." If it was, then keeping her residence in Colorado was a personal matter.

"When an assignment is truly temporary, it would be unreasonable to expect (a) taxpayer to move his home," the court said. His expenses are thus forced by the "exigencies of business."

(Six v. U.S.A., U.S. Ct. of Appeals, 2nd Cir., 1971.)
11/3/71

A court tosses out the IRS one-year rule on withholding taxes from per diems.

The IRS has ruled that if "temporary" job assignments go on a year or more, then per-diem allowances for meals and such become wages subject to withholding. A Houston engineering firm contested the point, however, and the Fifth Circuit appeals court recently ruled in its favor. The Houston outfit paid employes a living allowance while they worked on a Bartlesville, Okla., project. The job could be canceled on two weeks' notice, but it went on for four years.

The appeals court brushed aside the IRS ruling as "merely the opinion of a lawyer in the agency" and not binding. It also saw no basis for a one-year rule. "The payments are either wages or not from beginning to end." Wages are payment for services, the court recited, and it decided the living allowances weren't wages at all. The company paid employes the same allowance, whatever their base pay. It accounted for the payments separately, and it paid none to employes hired in Bartlesville.

Whether the payments were taxable income for the employes was another matter, the court said. But the company wasn't required to withhold taxes from them.

(Stubbs, Overbeck & Assoc. v. U.S.A., U.S. Ct. of Appeals, 5th Cir., 1971.)
7/21/71

Where's home? An employe can deduct living expenses incurred while working "away from home." The IRS recently argued that when a Boeing employe was assigned to Los Angeles for a year, that city became his home. (He had rented out his Seattle house and taken his family along.) But the Tax Court said a year's stint could be "temporary": It was long enough to bring the family but short enough to keep the house. And not selling the house was an important factor.

(Michaels v. Commissioner, 53 T.C. No. 28.)
11/26/69

No place like home? Normally traveling expenses

while away from home on business are deductible, but a district court recently denied a salesman's claim. The court said the deduction was meant to spare business travelers the burden of double living expenses. But this salesman had no "sleep-in, eat-in home" that cost him anything on a regular basis. He kept a few things at his brother's in Brooklyn, but that cost him nothing, and he spent almost all his time on the road.

(Rosenspan v. U.S.A., U.S. Dist. Ct., East. Dist. New York, 1970.)
4/22/70

Lawyers say that anyone who represents himself has a fool for a client. But last week, an elderly lady from Florida persuaded the Tax Court she deserved substantial deductions. A retired legal stenographer, she came to New York for seven months to find temporary work. It would be "highly unreasonable" to expect her to move her permanent home to New York, the court said. It let her deduct train fare and 32 weeks' lodging.

(Avery v. Commissioner, T.C. Memo. 1970-269.)
9/30/70

A carpenter sustained his claim to deduct living expenses while working "away from home," even though one of his job stints lasted 15 months. He couldn't find work in Colorado Springs, Colo., so he took jobs in nearby states. The Tax Court concluded that he maintained his home and personal ties in Colorado Springs, and all his jobs elsewhere qualified as "temporary."

(McGimsey v. Commissioner, T.C. Memo. 1971-124.)
6/2/71

The Commuter's Weary Road

Another decision on commuting continues the hard line of no deduction.

Few tax precepts are stricter than the rule that commuting isn't deductible. A recent Tax Court decision makes this rule even stiffer. It involved a Brooklyn, N.Y., consulting engineer who worked for two New York City firms that sold his services to still other companies. The man worked a 16-month stint at a Long Island company and eight months in Connecticut. He sought to deduct the expenses of his daily drive to the job.

The IRS denied the deduction because it claimed the jobs weren't temporary or far enough from home. The Tax Court went further and concluded that the engineer was simply a commuter. It said he worked for the New York firms "in form only." His job stints might be temporary, but that didn't transform his daily travel expenses into business transportation costs. "Commuting is commuting, regardless of the work, the distance traveled or the mode of transportation," the court said.

One judge dissented. He protested that the court was interpreting the law even more stiffly than the IRS.

(Turner v. Commissioner, 56 T.C. No. 3.)
4/28/71

The Tax Court bucks higher courts in fighting an exception for commuting tests.

Commuting costs aren't deductible, but two circuit courts (the Second and Seventh) have reversed the Tax Court and given deductions to taxpayers who had to carry bulky materials to work. Last week, the Tax Court ruled again on the issue and it restricted the exception to the narrowest possible circumstances. Otherwise, it said, "every person who lives in the suburbs and carries a brief case" could claim such a deduction. Nearly everyone incurs a cost in getting to work, the court said, and the flat rule of no deduction treats everyone the same.

According to the Tax Court, if a commuter would drive to work anyway, then carrying heavy tools or materials merits no deduction because he incurs no extra expense. And if the tools are the only reason for driving, the taxpayer must show that they are so heavy and bulky it's impractical to carry them on public transportation.

In one of three cases, the court nevertheless gave a deduction to a pilot who carried 40 pounds of gear but would have driven anyway. The case was within the Second Circuit, and the Tax Court applies a circuit court's views within that circuit, even when it disagrees.

(Fausner v. Commissioner, 55 T.C. No. 62.)
1/13/71

Things are tough all over, the Tax Court told a group of civilian employes at Vandenberg Air Force Base. It rejected their claim that at least part of their commuting costs should be deductible because they were required to live off-base. The court found their "hardships are no different than those confronting the many taxpayers who cannot find employment and must daily commute."

(Sanders et al. v. Commissioner, 52 T.C. No. 104.)
9/24/69

Commuting expenses have been ruled deductible in one instance by a district court. The case involved a Washington State couple who worked at the Hanford Atomic Project. No one is allowed to live at Hanford, so the court granted a deduction for mileage between the reservation and Richland, the nearest town. The court chose to rule without waiting for a higher court to pass on a 1969 Tax Court decision. That court denied a deduction for civilians who worked at Vandenberg Air Force Base but had to live off-base.

(Edmerson v. U.S.A., U.S. Dist. Ct., West. Dist. Wash., 1970.)
6/3/70

Short haul: A St. Louis physician had his main office at home, from which he set forth on his rounds of calls and to a second office. The IRS claimed that the cost of driving to his first call, and back from his last, should be nondeductible commuting expenses. "We do not agree," the Tax Court said. "When (the doctor) makes his first business stop at his main office in his home . . . his commuting is not by automobile."

(St. John v. Commissioner, T.C. Memo. 1970-238.)
9/9/70

Deductions for Employment Fees?

An employment fee paid to find a better job is deductible, the Tax Court says.

Deductions have been permitted for "fees paid . . . for securing employment," but the IRS has tended to split hairs over which "fees" actually qualify. Now, over six dissents, the Tax Court has ruled that the $3,000 a financial executive paid an executive placement agency was deductible as a business expense even though he already had a job and the fee was nonrefundable.

According to the court, the man was in the business of "being a corporate executive," and in an economy where executives hop from job to job, the expense was "ordinary and necessary from every realistic point of view." The outlay wasn't personal in nature, the court said, because it was directly related to producing income. The IRS had argued that only contingent employment fees warranted a deduction, but the court disagreed.

In concurring opinions, five judges indicated they would go even further. They scored a 1969 decision which had denied a deduction because the taxpayer had merely sought employment but failed to secure it.

(Primuth v. Commissioner, 54 T.C. No. 36.)
3/11/70

A job-seeker could deduct fees paid to a counseling group, the IRS rules.

In a similar situation last year, the IRS contested the deduction but lost in Tax Court. The current IRS ruling involves a taxpayer who paid a fee for a "basic psychological examination" and for counseling on whether he was likely to cut the mustard as an executive. The outfit also sent out job applications for him, and one letter led to a job. His fee was payable whether he landed a job or not, however.

The IRS ruled the fee deductible as a business expense and repeated its traditional distinction between expenses of securing a job (considered deductible) and those of merely seeking a job (nondeductible, the IRS says).

(Rev. Ruling 71-308.)
7/28/71

Employment fees: A higher court takes a traditional stance on deductibility.

In the tax standing of employment fees, nothing succeeds like success. The IRS has traditionally drawn a sharp line between fees paid in seeking employment and those paid in actually securing it. Only the latter have been deductible as a business expense. Recently the Tax Court appeared to be moving away from this position, but an appeals court has upheld the IRS stand.

The case involved an executive who paid $2,170 in nonrefundable fees and expenses to Frederick Chusid & Co. to help him find a job. He eventually found a new job on his own hook. Because he didn't obtain employment through Chusid, the IRS denied the deduction, and a circuit court agreed. "Under no theory" could the sum be deducted, it said. The firm didn't get him a job, and its fees weren't contingent on finding him one.

In one recent case, a man found a job through Chusid, and the Tax Court allowed the deduction. But it based its decision on broader reasoning than the distinction between seeking and securing. Five judges went even further in concurring opinions and said the distinction wasn't helpful.

(Morris v. Commissioner, U.S. Ct. of Appeals, 9th Cir., 1970.)
4/8/70

Employment fees: The Tax Court rules on a long-standing dispute.

The question is whether a fee paid to an employment agency is deductible as a business expense. The IRS historically has held that a fee is deductible if it leads to a new job, but isn't deductible if it doesn't. In 1970, three Tax Court decisions broadened the circumstances where fees are deductible. And the court now has nearly eliminated the IRS's distinction.

In the latest case, Leonard Cremona, an "administrator" for a small company, tried to deduct a $1,500 fee he paid an agency to help him find a similar position elsewhere. The IRS said no; he didn't get another job or even an offer. But the court ruled Cremona was "in the business of being an administrator" and the fee was "no less" a legitimate expense of that business "merely because" he didn't land a job. A Tax Court judge originally handed down the Cremona ruling in March, but it was recalled for a look by the full court.

There weren't any dissents, but in concurring opinions a few judges indicated the broader policy isn't limitless. Without being specific, they made clear that only fees legitimately related to searching for a new job would be deductible.

(Cremona v. Commissioner, 58 T.C. No. 20.)
5/17/72

Deductions for Business Entertainment?

It may be easier to deduct entertainment as a business expense.

The Court of Appeals for the Second Circuit has ruled the IRS is too strict in its requirements for documenting such an outlay. According to the tax code, a taxpayer must substantiate the expense (1) by adequate records, or (2) by "sufficient evidence" corroborating his own testimony. The IRS has insisted that "sufficient evidence" means a written statement, but the circuit court says that isn't essential.

To demand something in writing is the same as requiring "adequate records," the court said, and that would make the two requirements mean the same thing. The taxpayer's alternative would mean nothing. The court ruled in a case involving a New York surgeon who always bought lunch for interns and residents assisting him. He offered no proof of what he spent except testimony from a cafeteria cashier. That wasn't enough for the Tax Court.

The Second Circuit ordered the case back to the Tax Court for more testimony on the meal costs. "Oral testimony, properly corroborated" would do, the higher court said.

LaForge v. Commissioner, U.S. Ct. of Appeals, 2nd Cir., 1970.)
11/25/70

An easier rule for deducting entertainment makes no difference in its first test.

The Second Circuit Court of Appeals caused a stir

recently when it held the IRS too strict in requiring that business entertainment be documented to be deductible. By law, a taxpayer must substantiate such an outlay (1) by adequate records, or (2) by "sufficient evidence" corroborating his own testimony. If "sufficient evidence" had to be in writing, then the choice would be meaningless, the court said.

With this in mind, the Tax Court reconsidered another case where it denied a taxpayer a deduction, but the court stuck by its original decision. The case involved a television lighting designer who claimed he used his pleasure boat on business. The court reiterated that the man's guest book, which each guest signed his first time out, wasn't nearly sufficient. It also said that a list of alleged business guests was "merely another form" of the man's oral testimony.

The court gave no credence to vague testimony by the designer's secretary, and it said that testimony by two business associates established that they had been on board, but no more.

(Fiorentino v. Commissioner, T.C. Memo. 1970-344.)
12/30/70

Country club set: The Tax Court denies a deduction for food and drinks and dues.

An Alabama C.P.A. lost on a tax issue that comes up again and again even though the taxpayers hardly ever get to first base. Like many professionals, the C.P.A. tried to deduct his country club dues and part of his club expenses as business outlays to promote his practice. He argued that because his profession forbids advertising, it was necessary to use social contacts to drum up business. Most of the expenses came when he took his turn buying lunch or drinks after playing golf.

The Tax Court ruled he didn't prove the expenses were primarily for business, rather than personal. Beyond that, he didn't come close to substantiating the outlays as the law requires. He often played golf with clients, but that didn't prove the ties were more than friendships among professionals. Typically, foursomes were formed on the links, not set up in advance. This suggested that "friendship and camaraderie" were primary.

The C.P.A. contended that most of his outlays qualified as business meals. But the court didn't consider "the '19th hole' and the 'gin rummy table' . . . generally conducive to business discussion."

(Randall v. Commissioner, 56 T.C. No. 67.)
8/4/71

Business and pleasure don't mix, at least not to the Tax Court's satisfaction.

Twice recently the court ruled on the "oft-encountered combination of personal and claimed business elements," and it denied deductions both times. In one case, a North Carolina doctor, an avid golfer, earnestly regarded the links as a good spot to meet prospective patients or gather referrals. He had no records, but from a list of his 1966 golf rounds, he inferred that 60% of his club dues usually went for business purposes. But the court said that estimate fell far short of the strict record-keeping required for business entertainment.

(Ross v. Commissioner, T.C. Memo. 1970-110.)

In another case, a New York architect wanted to deduct landscaping expenses for a site he owned at Martha's Vineyard, where he had a summer place. He said he was building a showplace house to display his design abilities. There was a connection, the court conceded, but not enough to "transform the essentially personal character" of the project.

The house might be "commercially or professionally advantageous," but it was basically the same as a manufacturer showing off some of his products in his home.

(Page v. Commissioner, T.C. Memo. 1970-112.)
5/20/70

Bah, humbug! The Tax Court disallows the deduction of Christmas tips.

A New York City salesman of television time for ABC spread Christmas cheer in the form of $10 tips to office helpers, delivery boys, elevator starters, doormen and maitres d'. He sought to deduct the $160 total as a business expense. When challenged, he rebutted that the payments sped his deliveries, kept elevator doors open as he rushed up, and yielded better tables and quicker taxis.

The Tax Court flatly rejected the deduction for tips to office hands, delivery boys and elevator starters. The salesman had failed to show how these were even proximately related to his business, it said. The court conceded, however, that tips "on occasions too often to be mere coincidence" do secure a better table location or a taxicab more promptly. Such tips could reasonably be deducted, it said.

But it nevertheless turned down these deductions, too, because the salesman didn't give the documentation required for business entertainment expenses.

7/9/69

Expense accounts have a higher ceiling now. An employe who gets a fixed per diem for travel, entertainment or gift expenses isn't required to account in detail for the outlays unless the per diem exceeds the higher of $25 or 125% of the per diem the Government allows its employes. Recently President Nixon signed a measure raising the Federal figure to $25 from $16. That raises the ceiling to $31.25 for private businessmen.

11/26/69

No bonus: A lawyer gave his secretary $200 at Christmas, but the IRS refused to let him deduct more than $25 of it. The Tax Court agreed: Reasonable bonuses made in good faith are deductible, it said, but the lawyer didn't say the payment was anything more than a gift. Not until late—too late—in the trial did he raise the claim that the money was additional pay for services rendered.

(Steel v. Commissioner, T.C. Memo. 1969-254.)
12/10/69

Is It a Business Expense?

A fish story? A monger claims he had to make payments to customers' help.

When frozen fish came on the market, things turned rotten for New Amsterdam Fish Inc. and other New York City purveyors of fresh fish. Not only was the competing frozen product cheaper. In addition, the kitchen help at restaurants and hotels disliked fresh fish, which had to be "scaled, gutted, cleaned, deheaded, deveined, and portioned" before cooking, the Tax Court recited. Thus, the fresh-fish sellers worked out a system of cash "compensation" to relieve the kitchen help's distaste.

New Amsterdam claimed it regularly paid fishhandlers in its clients' kitchens 2% to 10% of their employers' monthly purchases. The firm said it routinely stuffed the cash in brown envelopes, which its salesmen distributed as they made their rounds. The sums came to $205,317 over four years and were debited to "sales commissions." The IRS smelled something fishy, however. It doubted the firm ever made such payments—or suspected the salesmen simply pocketed the money. But the Tax Court concluded the payouts were customary, the salesmen honest, and the payments real.

And if substantiated, the court said, there was no question they were deductible business expenses.

(New Amsterdam Fish Inc. v. Commissioner, T.C. Memo. 1971-17.)
1/27/71

The Cuban scene was a banker's Bay of Pigs, but Uncle Sam proved understanding.

An invesment banker urged customers, family and friends to invest in a plant that would make wallboard in Cuba. When the enterprise ran short of cash, the banker felt obliged to bail it out by arranging a bank loan. The loan was formally guaranteed by a closed corporation the banker and his brother owned, but in fact it rested on the banker's pledge that the debt wouldn't sour. When the infusion of money proved insufficient, the banker lent more, this time from his personal funds.

Along came Castro, who seized the business and lit his cigars with its IOUs. As good as his word, the banker ponied up to pay off the bank note the family corporation had backed. Then at tax time, he sought to deduct the payments as business expenses and the other money he lost as a business bad debt. The IRS balked; the personal loan wasn't part of investment banking, it said, nor was the banker liable for the corporation's guarantee.

The Tax Court was more sympathetic and allowed both deductions. The banker could reasonably believe that failure of the venture he had touted would hurt his own business, the court said. And by absorbing the bank note, the investment banker was protecting his reputation for business integrity.

(Milbank v. Commissioner, 51 T.C. No. 79.)
3/5/69

The big board takes care of its own, and the IRS rules it's deductible.

Since 1873, the New York Stock Exchange has maintained a "gratuity fund" to pay a death benefit to the family of a deceased member. The payment was doubled to $20,000 in 1930, and it hasn't been changed since. Last year, the fund was used 14 times, and at year-end, it stood at $540,000. This is the fund that Richard Whitney, Big Board president in the '30s, once tapped to cover his private loans.

A throwback to when the exchange was run as a private club, the fund is financed through nominally voluntary gifts. The exchange's 1,366 members pay $15 on joining and pledge to pay $15 more whenever a member dies. Last week, the IRS ruled that whatever the payments were called, they were deductible business expenses. A member "is bound to make such 'gifts' to maintain his standing," it said.

(Rev. Ruling 70-342.)
7/15/70

A lawyer claims politicking helps business, but the Tax Court is unimpressed.

Lawyers can't advertise, so they often go into politics instead. According to Martin Mayer's "The Lawyers," the neophyte who fails to run for office "may be suspect in the eyes of his colleagues—what other, sinister way does he have to find clients?" In a recent Tax Court case, a Florida attorney ran for the state senate and lost. He then tried to deduct about $7,200 in campaign outlays as ordinary and necessary business expenses.

Not only was it his duty to run for office, the attorney said, but the bar also urged its members to do so "as a practical means of 'advertising.' " But the Tax Court said his expenses were entirely personal. "He has not pointed to a single client obtained or a single fee received . . . as the result of his campaigning." It found only a "vague relationship" between the campaigning and his law practice.

(Maness v. Commissioner, 54 T.C. No. 155.)
8/19/70

Good government can merit an investment, a court says in a gift-tax case.

A decade ago, Mrs. Edith Rosenwald Stern, a wealthy Louisiana resident, gave $60,850 to support reform slates in New Orleans and statewide elections. She and her fellow contributors said they were disturbed by the state's lagging economy and considered the state's politics responsible. The money went for campaign literature and advertising. The IRS claimed the sums were gifts, however, and dunned her for $35,908 in taxes and interest.

Mrs. Stern contended she got full value for her money because she had a stake in better government. The tax law presumes that a transfer in the ordinary course of business is made for adequate consideration (and thus isn't a gift) if it's bona fide, at arm's length and free from donative intent. That's fine, the IRS said, but it denied the transfer was made in the course of "an actual business carried on by Mrs. Stern."

The Fifth Circuit appeals court said the IRS construed the law too narrowly. "The transfers were permeated with commercial and economic factors," it said. "In a very real sense, Mrs. Stern was making an economic investment."

(Stern v. U.S.A., U.S. Ct. of Appeals, 5th Cir., 1971.)
2/10/71

The IRS boosts auto mileage deductions for business use 20%.

The rate is being increased to 12 cents a mile from 10 cents, which has been allowed since 1966. The mileage allowance is an alternative to deducting actual operating expenses, and it applies to pick-up and panel trucks as well as automobiles. The mileage deduction can be claimed by businesses and self-employed persons and also by employes who use their cars on business without being reimbursed. The new rate is retroactive to tax years beginning Dec. 31, 1969, or after.

The IRS also is increasing the rate it recognizes for medical-expense deductions or charitable contributions to six cents a mile from five cents. If a taxpayer uses his car in charitable work or to drive to a doctor's office, he can claim the appropriate deduction. The business-use mileage rate is higher because it allows for depreciation.

With either the business rate or the charitable-medical rate, parking fees and tolls can be deducted separately.

(Rev. Procedures 70-24 and 70-25.)
10/14/70

A law firm can't expense legal fees it foots for some clients, the Tax Court says.

The case involved a California firm that specialized in personal injury cases, which it usually accepted for a share of any recovery won for the client. The law firm claimed that fierce competition for such cases forced it to bear many litigation costs (such as witness fees) itself—subject to repayment only if the client won the case and a monetary award. On its tax returns, the firm treated such outlays as expenses when incurred and as income if and when repaid.

The Tax Court sided with the IRS in denying that such costs were ordinary business expenses. The expectation of repayment meant the outlays were "in the nature of loans," the court said. It noted the firm's care in screening the clients it would accept on such a basis and also the firm's "good hopes" of being paid back. (Of the $6,925 the firm advanced in 1960, it recovered $6,233 within two years.)

The court also refused to allow a bad debt reserve in connection with cases still pending. It ruled that an "unconditional obligation" to repay didn't take effect until the cases were closed. If the money then proved uncollectible, the firm could make normal bad-debt deductions, the court said.

(Canelo v. Commissioner, 53 T.C. No. 23.)
11/19/69

Legal fees to fend off a suit weren't deductible, the Tax Court decides.

A case involving a wealthy Charlotte, N.C., woman concerned whether legal fees were deductible as expenses "for the management, conservation, or maintenance of property held for the production of income." The woman's home was burglarized, and she was attacked. She identified a suspect, who was indicted for burglary and rape. He was acquitted, however, and promptly sued her for malicious prosecution, asking $2 million in damages. The suit was thrown out, but the woman's legal bill came to $46,000.

The woman contended that if the suit were lost, then she would have lost most of her property, mainly stocks and bonds. Thus the outlay conserved property held for the production of income, she argued. But the Tax Court disagreed. Relying on a Supreme Court ruling, it said the deduction depended on whether the expenses were "in connection with the taxpayer's profit-seeking activities."

"It is perfectly clear," the Tax Court said, "that the circumstances which engendered the expenditures . . . were personal in nature."

(Brooks v. Commissioner, T.C. Memo. 1971-152.)
6/30/71

James B. Carey, the longtime Electrical Workers president, loses a Tax Court case.

The issue was whether Carey could deduct, as ordinary and necessary business expenses, about $16,000 he spent in his losing bid for reelection in 1964. The Tax Court said no, in part because it doubted that "common understanding in the ordinary affairs of life" would consider such outlays business expenses. It also leaned heavily on a Supreme Court case that denied a deduction to a state judge seeking reelection. "Powerful considerations of public policy" were invoked against the deduction.

The Tax Court decided the presidency of a large union involves "a comparable public policy element," but not all the court's judges agreed. Six would have denied the deduction but without getting into "public policy." Five others dissented. Carey, they said, was clearly "in the trade or business of being a labor leader," and campaign expenses were ordinary and necessary. "We must be realistic," the dissent declared. "Election expenditures are frequently the sin qua non of winning."

The courts have allowed a taxpayer to deduct the expenses of a corporate proxy fight, the dissent said. It considered that a better comparison than the case of the state judge.

(Carey v. Commissioner, 56 T.C. No. 36.)
6/23/71

An insider at General Motors has a decision reversed by a circuit court.

The case involved a GM vice president who sold 2,130 GM shares for $115,000 back in 1962 and then exercised an option to buy a like number of shares for $97,000. General Motors promptly claimed his $18,000 profit. By law, a short-term profit on the sale and purchase of a company's shares by an officer is collectible by the company. The executive paid up, and last year the Tax Court ruled he could deduct the full $18,000 as a business expense.

But the Sixth Circuit appeals court recently disagreed and called the payment merely a capital loss. According to the court, the taxpayer had received income that was taxed at reduced rates—the long-term gain on the 1962 sale of shares. Now he had to give up some of that income, and it was unfair for him to deduct the amount in full. If he did so, he would "enjoy preferred treatment twice."

(Mitchell v. Commissioner, U.S. Ct. of Appeals, 6th Cir., 1970.)
7/1/70

A coffee man's safaris were business trips but not grounds for deductions.

Dana W. Brown, former president of Manhattan Coffee Co., built up quite a reputation in coffee circles by showing movies he had taken on safaris to East Africa and other coffee-producing areas. The firm defrayed his expenses and built its advertising around his trips. But when Manhattan Co. changed hands, the new owners were less enthusiastic about the movies, which they felt mainly advertised Brown. He continued the safaris but paid for them himself.

The Tax Court recently ruled Brown couldn't deduct the outlays as ordinary and necessary business expenses. The trips were more than a hobby, it conceded, but they were "primarily" for enhancing his personal business reputation and "only incidentally" to boost Manhattan's sales. As such, the expenses were a capital outlay, akin to the costs of developing goodwill.

Normally the cost of capital assets is written off, and deducted, over their useful life. But there was no evidence that the useful life of his enhanced reputation could be ascertained, the court said. (On appeal, a circuit court was more direct: The trips couldn't be deducted as business expenses because Brown never proved they were necessary.)

(Brown v. Commissioner, T.C. Memo. 1970-253.)
9/16/70

Amend, brother, the Tax Court rules out a deduction for spiritual harmony.

Fred W. Amend, whose company makes Chuckles candy, fell into consulting a Christian Scientist before making many personal and business decisions. This spiritual guidance helped so much that Amend had his company put the man on retainer for consultation on business affairs. In 1965-66, he was paid $11,700, but the IRS wouldn't let it deduct the sum as a business expense.

The Tax Court found the question "vexatious" and "convoluted," but it upheld the Revenue Service. Even though the arrangement clearly aided Amend, "some expenses are so inherently personal they simply cannot qualify" as deductible business outlays, the court said. And what Amend sought wasn't business advice. It was "a state of harmony," reconciling his business thinking with spiritual beliefs.

(Amend v. Commissioner, 55 T.C. No. 31.)
11/25/70

Physician, depreciate thyself: The IRS takes a new view of human "useful life."

For many years, the IRS has routinely and rigidly rebuffed professional athletes, actors and others who sought to take write-offs on the gradual deterioration of their physiques or faces and thus their earning power. Outright amortization of the human body remains anathema, IRS officials say, but they've taken a step in that direction. They are permitting a doctor to use his life expectancy as the period for amortizing a hospital fee.

The doctor paid the fee for life-time, nontransferable privileges of practicing in a hospital he and other doctors organized. The IRS ruled the fee a capital outlay, rather than an immediately-deductible business expense. It purchased an intangible asset with a useful life of more than one year. Thus, the IRS concludes, the fee is "recoverable through amortization deductions based on a useful life equal to the taxpayer's life expectancy."

A "shorter useful life" could possibly be justified, the IRS adds. That presumably, refers to retirement plans rather than to anticipation of an untimely demise.

(Rev. Ruling 70-171.)
4/22/70

Little things mean a lot? A court won't quibble over small capital outlays.

Under the Internal Revenue Code, outlays on plant or equipment that last more than a year can't be deducted as current expenses. They must be capitalized and written off over the useful life of the asset. The code is hard and fast on this point, but businesses commonly ignore it for very small expenditures. The Treasury usually goes along, but there's no explicit statutory basis.

A recent Court of Claims decision may furnish some basis in case law, however. The decision involved a railroad that followed the old Interstate Commerce Commission rule permitting it to expense capital outlays less than $100. But when the ICC raised that limit to $500 some years ago, the Treasury balked.

The Court of Claims backed the railroad. The code's rule against expensing capital outlays isn't overriding, it said. The $500 rule was consistent with generally accepted accounting principles, the ICC said it didn't distort income, and, in dollar terms, it didn't make much difference, the court summarized.

Over 17 years, the $500 rule gave the railroad $230,000 in deductions, compared with $176,000 the IRS way. In context, that difference was "so minute as to become unfathomable," the court said.

(Cincinnati, New Orleans & Texas Pacific Railway Co. v. U.S., U.S. Ct. of Claims, 1970.)
4/29/70

Charles Wrightsman, who won a tax battle last year, may have lost the war.

The multimillionaire art collector won tentative reversal in 1969 of an IRS ruling that expenses of maintaining his collection—insured in 1967 for $16.8 million—weren't deductible. Wrightsman convinced a U.S. Court of Claims commissioner he and his wife had accumulated their art mainly as an investment, not a hobby. Some maintenance costs, therefore, were deductible as business expenses, the commissioner held.

Though it called the case "perplexing" and chided the IRS for shoddy reasoning, the full claims court upheld the Revenue Service. The Wrightsmans' deep personal involvement in their collection indicated pleasure rather than business was their primary motive, the court ruled. A dissenting judge said the couple's meticulous bookkeeping system, among other things, showed just the opposite.

The Wrightsmans may appeal the ruling to the Supreme Court, their lawyer says.

(Wrightsman v. U.S., U.S. Ct. of Claims, 1970.)
7/29/70

His first name is Walter. That was one of the disclosures when entertainer Liberace took the IRS to Tax Court. The principal issue was whether a corporation Liberace controlled could provide him with a $345,000 home and deduct the cost as a business expense. He lived there for a mere $300 a month, but the place also housed his production facilities, so the Tax Court more or less split the difference. It allowed one-half the corporation's claimed deduction, but it also ruled that Liberace had to include in his income one-half the home's fair rental value.

(International Artists Ltd. v. Commissioner, 55 T.C. No. 12.)
10/28/70

A teacher in Los Angeles paid out of his pocket for special equipment for his pupils to use. The Tax Court ruled that, as a matter of law, such outlays weren't deductible as business expenses. Recently, however, the Court of Appeals for the Ninth Circuit ruled that the lower court's decision "may be erroneous." It reversed the decision and ordered the case back to the Tax Court to give the teacher a chance to document his expenses.

(Patterson v. Commissioner, U.S. Ct. of Appeals, 9th Cir., 1971.)
2/3/71

A jury in a U.S. district court in Nebraska decided the IRS was wrong in disallowing an architectural firm's expenses in connection with its president's activities as head of a local civic organization. In doing so, the jury decided the president kept the company's name before the public by heading up the civic organization, and thus the expenses constituted "ordinary and necessary" business expenses.

(Leo Daly Co. v. Vinal, U.S. Dist. Ct., Dist. Nebr., 1968)
3/5/69

Downtown merchants get a boost from the IRS. The service advised it would permit merchants to deduct voluntary payments to city authorities to help develop public parking facilities near their businesses. The IRS promised similar treatment where merchants chipped in to remake a street. Their plans included ceramic tile sidewalks, a cobblestoned mall and continuous canopies. The city would own and maintain all the improvements.

(Rev. Rulings 69-85, 69-86, 69-90.)
3/12/69

A physician who raised 800 apple trees as a sideline was allowed by the Tax Court to deduct his losses on the operation even though the Revenue Service claimed that the trees may have had an aesthetic value but not a commercial value to him. The court said the size of the orchard suggested a business and agreed with the taxpayer's contention that "there's nothing aesthetic or pleasant about thousands of decaying apples on a 10-acre farm."

(Currie v. Commissioner, T.C. Memo. 1969-4.)
1/22/69

What's news? Mahlon H. Elliott, a Methodist minister in Alexandria, Va., was in a tax audit when the IRS auditor questioned the books and magazines he had taken deductions for. Why The Wall Street Journal? the IRS lady asked. Well, a clergyman has to know what's going on in the world, and the newspaper keeps him in touch, the minister said. The IRS lady denied the deduction. Mr. Elliott then asked about "Portnoy's Complaint," which the auditor allowed. Why the book but not the Journal? " 'Portnoy's Complaint' has social relevance, and the Journal doesn't," the IRS lady replied.

3/24/71

No contest: A couple carried off a $10,000 Better Homes and Gardens prize by redoing their attic as a recreation room in the style of a Victorian ice cream parlor. But while their prize was taxable, a circuit court recently turned down their claim that the $9,800 they spent on the job was an off-setting deductible expense. The money produced a permanent improvement, the court said.

(Paxman v. Commissioner, U.S. Ct. of Appeals, 10th Cir., 1969.)
8/20/69

Fat chance: An overweight airline pilot sweated off 38 pounds in two months to land a job with United.

He then sought to deduct $500 as a business expense, representing about two-thirds of what a new, slimmer wardrobe cost him. The Tax Court backed the IRS in refusing the deduction. It is well-settled, the court said, that only clothing required for employment but unsuitable for daily wear is deductible.

(Kennedy v. Commissioner, T.C. Memo. 1970-58.)
3/18/70

Abe Saperstein, the late owner of the Harlem Globetrotters, was upheld in a recent Tax Court case. Back in the early 1960s, he tried to set up the American Basketball League and lent it $56,000 in a fruitless effort to keep it alive. The IRS claimed the debt was merely personal, but the court allowed his estate to deduct the sum as a business bad debt: Saperstein had had a falling-out with the National Basketball Association, and he hoped the new league would assure his Globetrotters competition and access to arenas.

(Estate of Saperstein v. Commissioner, T.C. Memo. 1970-209.)
8/12/70

Back in the fifties, Consumers Power Co. of Michigan chipped in for an industry advertising campaign that extolled privately owned electric power companies over publicly owned. It also attacked the latter as "creeping socialism." Recently a circuit court denied Consumers Power a deduction for its outlays. They were an attempt to influence legislation, the court said, rather than an ordinary and necessary business expense.

(Consumers Power Co. v. U.S.A., U.S. Ct. of Appeals, 6th Cir., 1970.)
6/17/70

Life Is Very Taxing These Days (II)

April 15 sends some people to a psychiatrist rather than to an accountant.

Reactions to the annual ritual are "as specific to each person as his fingerprints," says Dr. Henry Krystal, a psychiatrist with Wayne State University. But "to the extent we harbor guilt, and we all do," he believes, "the income tax return mobilizes feelings of anxiety and vague self-accusation." Amassing wealth builds up guilt, Dr. Krystal declares, and some people assuage that guilt by paying more taxes than they actually owe.

Tax-paying can become a form of atonement through suffering, Dr. Robert Beavers, a Dallas psychiatrist, says. Psychoanalysts also report that emotional hang-ups can keep a person from filing. In one instance, a wealthy young woman had always relied on her "distant and frightening" father to handle money affairs. When the time came to handle her own, the trauma was too much. Her problem wasn't licked until she took her records to her analyst and "we spent an afternoon sorting them all out on the floor."

One "manic-depressive" Dallas businessman evaded all taxes. His business brought in up to $40,000 a year, which let him feel prosperous despite pressing financial concerns. "Filing a return would have destroyed the fantasy," his analyst explains. But severe depression overtook him when the IRS got him for tax evasion.

4/15/70

Dealing With the IRS

The IRS report gives the nitty-gritty on separating taxpayers from their money.

The IRS collected $195,722,096,497 in fiscal 1970, according to the commissioner's annual report, recently released. That's more than $962 for every man, woman and child in the United States. It's up 64% from $588 a head a mere five years earlier. In fiscal 1970, receipts from alcohol and tobacco taxes amounted to more ($6.84 billion) than total federal tax collections in 1940 ($5.34 billion).

It cost the Revenue Service 45 cents to collect each $100, it says. (The figure has been under 50 cents every year but one since 1950.) Of total collections, individual income taxes accounted for $103.65 billion, or 53%. About 54.4 million taxpayers, or two out of three who filed the 1040 Form, were due refunds, averaging $241 each. The IRS says that $32.86 billion in taxes, or 17% of the total take, was collected in New York State alone. California was a distant second with $18.60 billion.

The IRS says it ended fiscal '70 with 14,328 different forms or form letters in inventory. That's after adding 1,858 new ones and cutting out 2,897 old ones.

5/12/71

Here's a rundown on how things go when the IRS and a taxpayer disagree.

The IRS audited 2 million returns in fiscal 1970, well down from 2.5 million the year before. About 1.7 million were audits of individual or fiduciary income tax returns, which works out to about one in 47. In 1.2 million of the 2 million audits last year, additional taxes and penalties totaling $3.1 billion were assessed.

More than 98% of tax disputes are settled without going to court, the IRS says. Its internal appeals procedures disposed of 52,324 cases in 1970, compared with 1,313 cases decided by federal courts. Four out of five taxpayers who carry their cases to the IRS appellate division settle there, with settlements averaging 30% of the claimed tax deficiency. Of cases decided by the Tax Court, the IRS won 327, lost 82 and had 161 partly favorable and partly unfavorable decisions last year.

5/12/71

Why do taxpayers flock to private tax services when the IRS gives advice for free?

This year the IRS will have almost 1,300 full-time staffers, plus numerous temporary clerks, fielding taxpayers' questions. Yet private services boom. One Boston tax lawyer believes there's often scant difference in the quality of advice. A wage-earner with routine deductions "could go to the most expensive tax service or the Government man and wind up with about the same tax," he says.

Other tax advisers and taxpayers are considerably more dubious. Some complain of long waits, sketchily trained clerks, cut-and-dried treatment, and occasional surliness at the IRS. "They wouldn't take time to go over my proof," says Mrs. Dorothea Stibbs of Chicago. She says the IRS advised her against claiming a dependent that she subsequently claimed without challenge. But beyond such complaints, "people confronted with their tax return simply become flustered," says Henry Rush of Chicago Tax Service. "They come to us to take it off their hands."

Last year the IRS helped almost 29 million taxpayers. "The (private) tax preparer is going to sit down and prepare the return," an IRS spokesman says. "We more or less help you prepare your own."

2/18/70

Fear and mistrust channel many taxpayers to private tax return services.

"Do you honestly think I'd level with the IRS—or they'd level with me?" asks a 27-year-old music teacher in Evanston, Ill. Other taxpayers feel the IRS is unlikely to show them all the angles, and a private tax service will. Still, Business Control Service, a San Francisco firm, says it discourages many claims for deductions. "We don't want the client to get his finger caught in the ringer."

Does this mean many taxpayers are out to cheat? "No," replies Mrs. Elaine Mason, a tax adviser in Chicago. "People fear the IRS, and many even tend to be reluctant about (legitimate) deductions." One Chicago man turned down deductions that could have saved him $125. "I just don't want the tax people to investigate me," he declared.

2/18/70

Thirty million taxpayers may have the IRS compute their taxes due for 1970.

Under the rules, eligible taxpayers may fill in the rest of their returns, but have the IRS figure the tax. The IRS then dispatches a bill or a refund. The provision has been expanded to include taxpayers with incomes up to $20,000 who take the standard deduction and whose income comes from salaries and wages, dividends, interest, and—a newly eligible category—pensions and annuities. The IRS also will compute the retirement income credit for the elderly.

The Treasury has found that more people make mistakes in computing the tax than in any other part of the return. Assistant Secretary Cohen also has cited findings that 75% of those who receive pension or annuity income report it wrong. Most pay too much tax. And one-third of those eligible for the retirement income credit don't claim it because it's too complicated.

"I worry about the simplicity," Cohen has said, "not for the thousands who can afford expert (tax) advice, but for the millions who cannot and shouldn't be required to."

12/2/70

Failure to file: "An unsigned return is no return at all," the Tax Court rules.

The IRS assessed a Pennsylvania man with additional taxes of $17,500 and then socked him with a 25% penalty tax (5% a month, up to 25%) for failure to file. The taxpayer protested that he had turned in his return, together with a signed check for the $1,169 he thought due, but had "overlooked" signing the return.

The Tax Court agreed with the IRS that even with a signed check, an unsigned return wouldn't do. For one thing, signing a return normally makes a taxpayer subject to perjury proceedings if the information is false. The signature on a check wouldn't bring a person under this possible penalty, which the court considered "one of the principal sanctions available to assure that honest returns are filed." It didn't find willful failure to file but the oversight still meant a penalty.

(Vaira v. Commissioner, 52 T.C. No. 106.)
10/15/69

The IRS padlocked a premises and was ordered to pay rent as the occupant.

A U.S. district court came to the rescue of a party caught in the middle when the IRS moved against a delinquent taxpayer. The IRS seized the assets of a Chicago restaurant and locked up the premises until the assets were sold or released. (It took about a month.) That was all well and good, except the restaurant was also in arrears on its rent. A court had already awarded its landlord repossession, though the order had been stayed for 30 days.

The Revenue Service refused to pay the landlord rent, so he sued, and the court sided with him. It decided that by its actions, the IRS had "implicitly agreed and contracted" to pay the reasonable value for use and occupancy of the place. The court awarded the landlord a month's rent ($1,300), plus interest and legal costs.

When the IRS padlocked the place, that amounted to a "condemnation of (the landlord's) rights and property without just compensation," the court said.

(Weber v. U.S.A., U.S. Dist. Ct., No. Dist. Illinois, 1970.)
6/2/71

Estimated tax payments were due yesterday—amid some confusion.

A great many taxpayers are legally obliged to file a declaration of estimated taxes, but many boast they've never filed and believe the IRS doesn't care. The IRS contends that isn't so. There's no penalty simply for failure to file, it says, but the penalty of 0.5% a month for underpaying an installment is automatic, it insists. Exceptions to the provision are liberal, however, and many nonfilers aren't subject to penalty.

By law, a taxpayer must file if his tax for 1971 is estimated to exceed his withholding by $40 or more, and (a) his income not subject to withholding exceeds $200, or (b) his income exceeds a certain figure ($5,000 for single taxpayers). If a taxpayer's tax will come to $9,000 and his withholding to $7,000, he should pay the other $2,000 in quarterly installments. But if at each installment date, he has paid 80% of the amount due by that date, there's no penalty. And the law provides four different ways to estimate the tax and avoid the penalty.

During fiscal 1970, only 7.4 million taxpayers filed declarations, the IRS says. It has no count of how many were penalized for underpayment.

6/16/71

Helping hand? A Massachusetts woman got some free assistance from the IRS in preparing her 1967 return. Later, when the IRS challenged her deductions, she expressed "surprise and annoyance." The Tax Court found her chagrin understandable, but it ruled against her on every count. According to the court, the IRS "informally" helps millions of taxpayers a year, and its employes "cannot be expected to be correct as to every question asked or held to a standard of infallibility," especially when they may not know all the facts.

(Stokes v. Commissioner, T.C. Memo. 1970-200.)
8/5/70

High cost of filing: A computer study coughs out the estimate that taxpayers' efforts in filling out Federal returns for 1967 were worth some \$1.3 billion. The study is one of a series for the American Bar Foundation. It bases its estimate on what a tax service would have charged to complete the returns, plus \$10 an hour for a taxpayer's time in drawing together the data.

6/25/69

Most tax disputes are settled by officials within the taxpayer's IRS district, the IRS says. When the IRS calls taxpayers in for an audit, and they disagree with its results, the first step in a chain of appeals is a conference with the district director's representative. (A handful of cases start at a higher IRS level or go directly to the courts.) Of the disputes that go to a district conference, better than seven out of 10 are resolved there without further ado, the IRS says.

12/23/70

Turnabout: A taxpayer reached a compromise with the IRS, paid the tax, then sued for a refund. The IRS then decided to take another look at his return and said it had additional taxes in mind. The taxpayer sought an injunction to bar the IRS from reopening the case after an agreement had been reached. But a U.S. district court ruled the taxpayer had rejected the agreement by going to court, and the IRS was entitled to as much. "Otherwise, the matter would be a one-way street," the court declared.

(Crocker v. U.S.A., U.S. Dist. Ct., No. Dist. Miss., 1971.)
6/23/71

Summer help and part-time workers may avoid having taxes withheld from paychecks. Effective May 1, the exemption is open to anyone who certifies he had no taxes due for last year and expects none due for this year. The IRS believes the provision will affect about six million persons, mainly students who work during vacation. Under 1970 rates, a single person who makes less than $1,725 owes no tax. That's based on a personal exemption of $625 and the $1,100 low income allowance. If a qualified employe requests an exemption, the employer has no choice in the matter.

(IRS News Release No. 1033, 1970.)
4/15/70

Farm and household workers may ask to have income taxes withheld from their pay, under regulations recently made final by the IRS. An employe can make the request by filing Form W-4 with his employer, the IRS says, but the voluntary withholding can't proceed unless the employer agrees.

(IRS News Release IR-1118, 1971)
3/24/71

The short form 1040A's being dropped greatly increased the proportion of low-income people itemizing deductions. Total returns with incomes under $5,000 for 1969 fell by about one million, but the number of such returns with itemized deductions jumped one million. The 1040A only permitted a standard deduction, and many low-income people lost deductions they could claim if itemized.

10/21/70

By the book: IRS Commissioner Thrower suggests that the Revenue Service take a tip from Robert Townsend's bestseller, "Up the Organization." Townsend said no executive should approve a new form without first filling it out himself. A great idea, the IRS staff replied —so good it had been suggested a number of times in the past. So why hasn't it already been applied to working out new tax forms? Well, Thrower was the first commissioner to suggest it, he was told.

7/1/70

Valediction: Retiring IRS Commissioner Thrower says he will leave office with "a special and deep affection" for Form 1040. "The trials of little Eva on the ice wouldn't compare with those of Form 1040," he declares. According to Thrower, the IRS considered its new 1040 a first-rate achievement. "We sat back and waited for the applause," he says, but the acclaim was hardly overwhelming. Thrower discovers a lesson in this for his successor, whoever he may be: "Keep trying, but you can't win."

5/5/71

Ah, progress: Edwin S. Cohen, Assistant Treasury Secretary for tax policy, marvels over IRS prowess in using computers. Still, he was disturbed to find that the computers sent him two sets of 1040 forms, one to his current address and the other to his Charlottesville, Va., home. Cohen wasn't eager to pay his taxes twice, so he asked the IRS computer people to fix things up. Sorry,

Cohen says he was told, there was no way to correct the error because it was impossible for it to have happened.

5/5/71

Appraising art has always been a bane for the IRS, which at times finds more creativity in the donor's tax return than in the art work he gives away. In 1968 the IRS set up a panel of experts to appraise works involved in tax disputes. Since then, the panel has looked at 300 works, for which donors claimed deductions totaling $35 million. The panel chopped that figure by $10 million. In estate tax cases, where higher values mean higher taxes, it boosted values to $7 million from $2 million.

11/4/70

Revenuers reorder their priorities as tides of crime shift. The IRS reports confiscating 1,799 illegal stills in the latter half of 1970, down from 1,939 a year earlier. But its Alcohol, Tobacco and Firearms Division boosted seizures of "destructive devices" to 799 in the same months, up from a mere 60 a year before.

2/17/71

Baring one's soul? In Amsterdam, an aggrieved taxpayer entered a tax office, stripped to the buff, put his clothes on the counter and shouted, "Take it all then!" He stalked out, but was later persuaded to return for the clothes and a mental examination.

2/25/70

How wordy is the tax law? Edwin S. Cohen, Assistant Secretary of the Treasury, gave an indication in discussing a pending piece of legislation. The proposal would substitute the word "Secretary" wherever the phrase the (Treasury) "Secretary or his delegate" appears in the law. Then in one place "Secretary" would be defined as including his delegate, too. That change, Cohen says, would shorten the Revenue Code by about 5,000 words.

2/3/71

Washington tax lawyers note that a major revamping of the tax law apparently comes along every 15 years, for example in 1939, 1954 and 1969. They're already bracing for the next round—in 1984.

5/5/71

Your Day in Tax Court

The tax court says it will defer to individual circuit court views.

Though it can be reversed by any one of 11 appeals courts, the Tax Court has considered itself a national court and sought to apply its thinking uniformly in all areas of the country. Reversal by an appeals court hasn't been binding on the Tax Court as a precedent in future cases. As a result, when the Tax Court and a circuit court disagreed, a litigant could expect to go through a losing bout in the Tax Court before winning on appeal.

In two recent cases, however, the Tax Court said it intends to respect a circuit court's rulings in cases arising in its circuit. "Better judicial administration requires us to follow (such a) decision which is squarely in point where appeal from our decision lies to that court and that court alone," the lower court said. This opens the way for it to rule one way in one circuit and another way in a second circuit.

The Tax Court noted it can still follow its own bent when the circuit court hasn't spoken. Even when it has, the Tax Court can indicate its own disagreement, it says.

(Golsen v. Commissioner, 54 T.C. No. 70.)
4/29/70

The Tax Court gears up for its new Small Tax Case Division.

The division was authorized by the Tax Reform Act and is limited to tax disputes involving up to $1,000 for any one taxable year or in estate taxes. Taxpayers may hire lawyers to represent them, but, in most cases, the stakes would be too small. The small-case procedures are geared to taxpayers representing themselves. Recently the court put out a simplified five-question form that will serve as a petition to the court. The forms will be available about Dec. 15 from the U.S. Tax Court, Box 70, Washington, D.C. 20044.

Four commissioners have already been appointed to handle the small cases, supervised by a Tax Court judge. The new division won't take full effect until Dec. 30, but the commissioners have already been assigned cases under interim rules. The court has scheduled small-case calendars in 11 cities next January to March and in 17 next April through June. The idea, Chief Judge Drennen says, is "to give the small taxpayer a fair, fast, informal, and inexpensive hearing close to home."

According to the court's new rules, "any evidence deemed by the court to have probative value" will be admissible in small cases, which are to be conducted "as informally as possible."

10/29/70

Small claims channels at the U.S. Tax Court are busy but not flooded.

Since last fall, commissioners, rather than judges, have handled small tax cases under simplified procedures. These permit taxpayers to argue their own causes in tax disputes involving $1,000, or less. The commissioners' decisions can't be appealed. Thus far the five commissioners have held sessions in 31 cities and were assigned 1,337 cases. Of those, 965 were settled before trial. Forty-one were dismissed when the taxpayers didn't press them. Two hundred have been continued, and only 131 actually have gone to trial.

At trial, many more taxpayers lose than win. The small cases include "a fair number of hopeless causes," says Chief Judge William M. Drennen of the parent Tax

Court. Many taxpayers don't grasp what they must do to prove their point, even under relaxed rules of evidence. Others push "a concept of what the law should be, rather than what it is," says Judge Howard A. Dawson Jr., who supervises the Small Tax Case Division.

At 2,400 a year, the small cases are no more numerous than before the special rules were set up. But Judge Dawson says the new channel has prodded the IRS into settling more disputes out of court.

7/21/71

Too many taxpayers miss the Tax Court's deadlines, the court says with distress.

If a taxpayer intends to contest a tax bill in the Tax Court, the law requires that he file a petition with the court within 90 days from when the notice of deficiency was mailed to him by the IRS. According to the court, it's had to toss out an increasing number of petitions because they weren't filed in time. Some petitioners misread the 90 days as three months, or as beginning on receipt of the notice.

The blunder is made most often by taxpayers representing themselves, Chief Judge William M. Drennen says. He has no exact count of how many cases have been rejected. "Whether there's an increase or a decrease, there are too many of them," he declares, "and I'd like to get the word out." The court must get the petition within the 90 days, or the petition must be correctly addressed, mailed and postmarked before the period runs out.

12/10/69

An Indian gets his day in court, but still no answer to his troubled "Why?"

Gordon Wallace Dymond Jr., an American Indian, went to Tax Court after the IRS assessed him for filing no returns for five years. He claimed the IRS erred in trying to force him "to voluntarily pay Federal taxes into a governmental structure whose overall objective he finds incomprehensible." Dymond asked for "conscientious objector" status, "so that I could maintain my convictions officially even while being forced to part with my material acquisitions."

"I find the thought of financially supporting something which I do not understand to be less than wise," Dymond said. He felt "these IRS Caucasians" were trying to impose their values on him by force. If the IRS tried reason, chances are he would pay up, Dymond said. Unfortunately, "the average citizen cannot understand me or my values until such time as this citizen understands his own." And in Dymond's view, most white Americans don't.

According to Dymond, the IRS told him he could put his views in a letter, but it would probably be disposed of because it "interfered" with the computer records. The Tax Court heard Dymond out, then ruled for the IRS. "He has selected the wrong forum," the court said.

(Dymond v. Commissioner, T.C. Memo. 1970-277.)
10/14/70

If you deal with the IRS, better keep it posted on your latest address.

If the IRS notifies you it thinks you owe it more taxes, an appeal to the Tax Court must be filed (or postmarked) within 90 days of when the IRS mailed its notice of deficiency. If a taxpayer misses that deadline, the court has no choice but to dismiss his appeal for want of jurisdiction. In two recent cases, taxpayers missed the 90-day mark, but blamed it on the IRS for sending its notice to the wrong address.

Neither taxpayer got very far. Both had indeed moved, but neither, the Tax Court ruled, had officially let the IRS know. In one case, a California woman's lawyer mentioned to an IRS man that she had moved, but the court didn't think that was enough. In the other case, the taxpayer wrote one IRS agent he was moving, but that agent was looking into his 1967 return. The man said nothing about all other tax mail, so the notice didn't count for a separate proceeding involving his 1966 return.

Anyone who claims the IRS notice went to the wrong address must show he filed "a clear and concise notification concerning a definite change of address," the court reiterated.

(Stewart v. Commissioner, 55 T.C. No. 22, and McCormick v. Commissioner, 55 T.C. No. 17.)
11/18/70

Canceled: If a taxpayer appeals an IRS "notice of deficiency" to the Tax Court, his petition must be received, or postmarked, within 90 days. In one recent case a New Yorker swore he mailed his petition on time, but the envelope showed up with no postmark at all. Dismissing the petition, the court declined to accept other evidence that the petition was mailed on time. "The risk of postmarking is on the taxpayer," it declared.

(Rappaport v. Commissioner, 55 T.C. No. 71.)
2/10/71

Dead letter: A Massachusetts couple mailed off a petition to the Tax Court within the 90-day period set by law, but unfortunately they mailed it to the IRS. By the time the letter was returned, the couple had missed the deadline for the Tax Court. The court ruled it couldn't accept the petition because the law clearly says it had to be filed "with the Tax Court" within the allotted period.

(Garland v. Commissioner, T.C. Memo. 1971-79.)
4/28/71

Time flies: Every calendar day counts, the Tax Court ruled, in figuring the deadline for a taxpayer's appeal of an IRS assessment to the court (150 days for petitioners abroad, 90 days for others). A taxpayer argued the law meant business days, by which count her petition arrived on time. But the law merely says the appeal period can't end on a Saturday, Sunday or holiday, the court concluded.

(McGuire v. Commissioner, 52 T.C. No. 50.)
6/25/69

Faraway places: A taxpayer assessed with a deficiency normally has 90 days to appeal to the Tax Court, but 150 are allowed if he's outside the U.S. Recently a California taxpayer claimed the extra time because, coincidentally, the day the notice was mailed to him, he spent about 10 hours across the border in Tijuana. The court conceded the law made no distinction between residence abroad and a temporary stay, but it still found his claim far-fetched.

(Cowan v. Commissioner, 54 T.C. No. 60.)
4/8/70

Time will tell if privately-metered mail meets Tax Court deadlines. Normally, the court accepts petitions by mail if postmarked before the period for appeal expires. But as private-meter postmarks aren't authoritative, such letters must also take no longer than usual in transit. Recently, the IRS acquiesced in the court's acceptance of a South Carolina petition mailed late on a Thursday (the deadline) and received in Washington the following Monday. But the court rejected a New York petition that took six days. The petitioner couldn't prove mail delays were to blame.

(Fishman v. Commissioner, 51 T.C. No. 86.)
4/2/69

Our "Voluntary" Tax System?

The IRS frets that voluntary compliance in paying taxes may be slipping.

A certain amount of hand-wringing is to be expected because it's time to ask Congress for money, but top IRS officials are expressing unusual concern. Commissioner Randolph W. Thrower has told Congress that signs point to "serious noncompliance in every tax area." According to Donald Bacon, assistant commissioner for compliance, the 1968 curbs on federal employment may well have left a lasting dent in voluntary compliance. "Audit coverage has declined to low levels," Treasury Secretary John Connally told Congress last week.

An IRS survey of 400 taxi drivers found that every last one had either underreported his income or failed to file, Bacon says. In one city, the IRS turned up "industry-wide collusion" in the hairdressing business to underreport employes' earnings. The IRS is also discovering problems with large, publicly owned corporations, Bacon says. There will always be "honest differences" over interpreting the tax law, he says, but the IRS is turning up underpayments that "go well beyond professional judgment or prudent tax planning."

Bacon also chafes mildly at having to divert so many IRS agents to work on organized crime. Such investigations require six times as much time as investigating "our 'legitimate' tax evaders," he quips.

5/5/71

The IRS revives its dismay over gross disparities in penalties for tax fraud.

According to the IRS, it's something like Monopoly: Land on the wrong square and you go to jail. Last week, Chief Counsel Worthy noted that in the Western District of Tennessee, 22 of 24 persons convicted of criminal tax offenses drew prison sentences. In the Western District of Virginia, one in 36 was jailed.

Such contrasts have persisted for years and seem no better now, Commissioner Thrower said earlier this year. In the First Circuit, prison sentences run 65%, but in the Third, only 18%. In the Fifth Circuit, the three Florida districts average about 50%; the three Georgia districts, less than 6%. The Federal district courts in New Jersey impose prison terms in about 2% of tax convictions.

No one can explain very well why some districts fall one way and some the other. In fact, Thrower contends such disparities continue in the face of a consensus among authorities that incarceration is essential to deter potential offenders. The IRS views tax fraud as a singularly rational, calculated crime—and singularly corrosive in a tax system based on trust.

"But for the ultimate threat of imprisonment, the odds for cheats could look very good," Thrower said.

12/9/70

Jail terms for tax offenders often prove easier in theory than in practice.

There he stands, a reputable citizen, with solid family, community and business ties—and a convicted tax cheat. "No other duty causes more sleepless nights" than sentencing such a man, a Federal judge once said. Tax offenders rarely repeat, and their records are otherwise clean. They have suffered through uncertainty and been shamed by exposure.

About 75% of the Federal judges polled for the Practising Law Institute said they believe prison terms deter potential tax violators. But many judges are obviously loath to send such a man to jail.

Perplexities exist on both sides. One judge asks whether tax compliance is actually better in districts where tax evaders go to jail than in those where they don't. But in the view of one judge, short sentences (or none) for tax offenders "supply ammunition for those who would claim our law discriminates against the poor."

12/9/70

To err is all too human, the IRS discovers. In fiscal 1970, one taxpayer in 12 had a math error on his return, but as in past years, the mistakes weren't distributed randomly. About 2.8 million taxpayers made errors that cost them money, a total of $212 million. But fully 4.2 million made mistakes in their own favor. Had their errors gone undetected, they would have cost the government $507 million.

5/12/71

Bar behind bars? The IRS says the legal profession tops its "most wanting" list.

"As a lawyer," IRS chief counsel Worthy said recently, "I am ashamed to say that in recent years more lawyers have been convicted of tax fraud than members of any other profession." During 1966-70, 224 lawyers were indicted for tax fraud and 203 convicted. Next worse among professionals were doctors and dentists (170 indicted and 154 convicted), followed by certified public accountants (42 indicted and 36 convicted). Total convictions ran 2,533, but the IRS says it has no breakdown for nonprofessional occupations.

Another trouble spot is small, closely held corporations, the IRS says. One IRS district recently ran intensive audits on 42 such firms. None had been audited in five years, and all consistently reported operating losses. The results: Twenty-seven of the firms (and 21 of their officers) had underpaid taxes by significant amounts. "Most shocking," according to Worthy, was that the audits turned up 11 probable instances of outright tax fraud.

The IRS says that sample was too small to merit any general conclusions, but it contends that small, closely held firms are a perennial tax problem. "There's more room for finagling," the IRS says.

12/16/70

The IRS finds widespread underreporting in certain doctors' and dentists' returns.

Goaded by a flap some months ago before the Senate Finance Committee, the IRS has checked the returns of about 8,400 individuals, mainly doctors and dentists, who received $25,000 or more in Medicare or Medicaid fees in 1968. The IRS assessed additional tax in more than half the cases, it says, and in such cases, the underpayments averaged $2,800. There were 47 cases of possible tax fraud.

The 8,400 taxpayers averaged $107,300 in total receipts, and they paid an average of $23,100 in taxes, the IRS says. About 15% of the taxpayers underreported their gross receipts, but such underreporting came to only 1% of total gross receipts for the group. Similarly, the IRS says, about four taxpayers in 10 underreported their net profits, but this involved only 3% of total net profits for the group.

The IRS notes pointedly that its findings don't necessarily hold true for "the entire health care profession."

5/19/71

How much money is stashed away in Swiss banks to evade U.S. income taxes?

A whopping $5 billion in the last four years is the

estimate pieced together by Arie Kopelman, a New York tax lawyer and UN consultant. Kopelman says his estimates are "admittedly incomplete," but he offers them as "very well supported hypotheses." They are based on something called the "errors and omissions" account in balance-of-payments figures.

That account covers money that shows up in one country without being recorded as leaving another. Tourist spending and cash sent to relatives abroad are entries, but studies suggest that short-term capital flows (which include bank deposits) are most important. Kopelman finds that over the last 10 years, the U.S. has had an enormous $12.86 billion deficit in errors-and-omissions with Switzerland. Much of this was normal commercial deals handled through Swiss banks, he says, but allowing for this still leaves billions in an unexplained flow of funds in 1966-69.

"The great bulk" of these billions is quite likely tax-evasion money, Kopelman contends. A U.S. Treasury aide says it has made no estimate, but adds that Kopelman's is "certainly not unthinkable."

11/11/70

Our tax system relies on "voluntary compliance," the IRS says, but it clearly works best when the IRS knows how much a taxpayer has earned, and he knows it knows. Compliance is much lower when the IRS lacks such independent verification, the IRS finds. It points out that back in 1963, the first year it got information returns on payments of interest, returns with interest income leaped 45% and the amounts reported jumped 28%.

2/24/71

How Much Did He Really Earn?

An attorney offers some tips on countering an IRS reconstruction of income.

If the IRS suspects tax evasion, it may try to reconstruct a taxpayer's income by the "net worth" method. That simply assumes that an increase in net worth, plus nondeductible outlays but minus nontaxable income, equals taxable income. Obviously, attorney Jeffrey W. Loubet says in Taxes magazine, the IRS must have a sound figure for initial net worth. Thus the first defense step is to judge whether the IRS can come up with such a figure on its own.

After that, Loubet says, it's a common ploy to try to explain away a net-worth increase by claiming the IRS initially overlooked a large cash hoard. But the taxpayer's standard of living or his previous income might belie that. Loubet says it's essential for the taxpayer to avail himself of the "inherent uncertainties" in the circumstantial net-worth method. Often if he catches the IRS in "one or two flagrant errors," that's enough to discredit its entire computation, Loubet says. The taxpayer should also search for unclaimed deductions to offset any unreported income the IRS turns up.

According to Loubet, the courts have held that if the IRS substitutes its figures for a taxpayer's return, it assumes a heavy burden of proof. Thus, he says he feels the taxpayer will always win "the borderline case in criminal fraud" where the net worth method is used.

12/30/70

Shave and a haircut, four towels—by the Tax Court's count of a barber's income.

The IRS will devise practical means of checking a

taxpayer's income, and the courts will be no less practical in reviewing them. A St. Louis man ran a small barber shop but apparently learned all his bookkeeping in barber college. His ledgers were poor, so the IRS counted the towels he used, figured how many haircuts and shaves he gave, and estimated his income.

The Tax Court took the IRS figure, trimmed it all around and took a little off the top. "This method is not unreasonable," it said, but "it must be used intelligently." The IRS had overlooked that a shave took three towels to a haircut's one. It also forgot the barber didn't charge for some trims. Finally, the court discounted IRS testimony that at times the barber used the same towel twice. "Any barber who stuffed a towel full of hair" down a customer's neck wouldn't last very long, it said.

(Newton v. Commissioner, T.C. Memo. 1970-103.)
5/20/70

Wouldn't you know the IRS could find a use for the rising cost of living?

If a taxpayer isn't reporting income, the IRS has an arsenal of ways to construct its own figure. These range from counting towels in a bordello to checking published trade data on the average mark-up of a jewelry store. Last week still another method passed muster at the Tax Court. The IRS estimated a convicted bookie's income by using Labor Department cost-of-living figures, plus a percentage increase each year to allow for inflation.

The bookmaker challenged the method as "arbitrary and excessive," but the Tax Court disagreed. The IRS had reason to believe the man was earning money from bookmaking, yet he filed no returns and also refused to cooperate with the revenue agent. The court noted that Congress laid down no guidelines on determining tax liability, and that suggested it meant the IRS to have "great latitude."

Thus it was reasonable to use the Bureau of Labor Statistics figures, especially since the man couldn't explain what he lived on.

(Giddio v. Commissioner, 54 T.C. No. 145.)
8/5/70

Bank deposits that a couple can't explain lead to tax troubles.

If a taxpayer's bank account opened the year with $1,412, chalked up $239,283 in deposits, and contained $7.49 at year-end, how much did the taxpayer earn that year? About $224,590 more than he declared on his tax return, the IRS answered. Wrong, the Tax Court ruled. Actually, the man and his wife were kiting checks, it said. At least $184,078 in deposits merely reflected one check written to cover another falling due.

In this case, the IRS had questioned the couple's income and applied a method known as "bank deposits and cash expenditures" to make its own estimate. The taxpayer, a blind attorney, protested that in fact they were badly in debt and making payments to 10 lenders. In a desperate effort to keep up, they "availed themselves" of the time lag between when a check is cashed and when it is presented for payment. They devised at least eight ways to cash a check somewhere and make a quick deposit before previous checks bounced.

The Tax Court drastically chopped the IRS estimate, but it still found $34,889 in deposits and cash outlays unexplained. A federal appeals court went even further. It ruled the couple had no unreported income whatsoever and in fact was due a $197 tax refund.

(Teichner v. Commissioner, U.S. Ct. of Appeals, 2nd Cir., 1972.)
11/25/70

A swindler in the great salad oil scandal bests the IRS in Tax Court.

Before the bubble burst for Allied Crude Vegetable Oil Refining Corp., Ben Rotello had the chore of spreading bribes to keep the Anthony DeAngelis operation afloat. He drew checks against "petty cash" to pay bank clerks and New York dockworkers to give Allied Crude special treatment. Later he bribed a clerk at Bunge & Co., a creditor, to delay depositing Allied's remittances. Still late, he paid the clerk thousands of dollars to substitute Allied's ordinary checks for certified checks it had sent Bunge.

A Federal court sentenced Rotello to three years for his part in the swindle. When the IRS sifted the financial wreckage, it charged that Rotello had failed to report $139,000 in taxable income. The IRS claimed he had cashed or endorsed that sum in petty cash checks, with no evidence that the money was in fact used for business purposes. Rotello denied taking a cut, but the IRS said he couldn't be believed.

But the court believed him anyway. It found the pattern of under-the-table payments entirely plausible, and it saw no evidence that Rotello had lived beyond his means.

(Rotello v. Commissioner, T.C. Memo. 1970-213.)
8/5/70

A "friendly favor" raises IRS suspicions of squirreling away untaxed cash.

The IRS socked a Chicago woman with a $3,700 tax deficiency, based largely on a report from her bank that she had changed $10,000 in small bills. The bank's records also showed she had entered her safe deposit box the same day. The woman owned a restaurant, and the IRS concluded she was stashing away part of her profits.

The woman was in a pickle, but the Tax Court accepted her explanation: She had encountered an acquaintance who wanted to change the money but lacked a bank account. She had helped him, but had never seen him again. Her financial records and living standard were consistent with this, the court said, and it was impressed with her accountant's testimony on her behalf.

(Collins v. Commissioner, T.C. Memo. 1970-91.)
5/6/70

Bridge expert Oswald Jacoby didn't report $203,000 from gambling, a court finds.

The IRS claimed that Jacoby and his wife had more than $268,000 in unreported income during 1960-64, mainly from betting on cards, dice and sports (but not tournament bridge). Twice the couple filed no return at all. The IRS used their bank deposits and cash expenditures to reconstruct their income. But the Jacobys protested that his losses at least equaled his winnings. "Mr. Jacoby is a compulsive gambler," his wife testified. "If he would only follow what he writes in his books, he would be as winning a player in anything . . . as he is in bridge tournaments."

The Tax Court trimmed the IRS figure, but it basically upheld the Revenue Service. It did find, however, that Jacoby indeed had substantial gambling losses. "We are convinced (Jacoby) gambled frequently, compulsively, and unwisely," the court said. But it recognized only $139,000 in deductible losses because Jacoby had no records other than hundreds of cancelled checks.

Jacoby's "modest" scale of living indicated heavy losses. He enjoyed few of the luxuries that "would normally flow from (his) writings, his individual genius, and his gross gambling receipts," the court said.

(Jacoby v. Commissioner, T.C. Memo. 1970-244.)
9/9/70

Is It Fraud?

Failure to file isn't tantamount to tax fraud, the Tax Court decides.

An Oregon lawyer, a former assistant U.S. Attorney who once prosecuted tax cases, found himself on the other side of the fence. He pleaded guilty in 1967 to willful failure to file returns for 1961 through 1964. He claimed he failed to file for 1961 because he lacked the money to pay his taxes. Then he became afraid that filing later returns would give away his omission and possibly cause him to be disbarred. When the IRS caught up with him, he had all four returns in various stages of completion.

The Tax Court was asked whether the 50% penalty for civil tax fraud should apply. It noted that willful failure to file isn't necessarily fraud, but merely one fact to consider along with "other relevant facts." "Admittedly, this is a close case," the court said, but it concluded the lawyer intended ultimately to pay his taxes. He cooperated fully with the IRS and made no effort to hide what he owed.

The lawyer was "caught in a web of his own making," the court declared. But "a failing in judgment and character cannot be equated with intent to defraud," it said.

(Morrell v. Commissioner, T.C. Memo. 1971-99.)
5/12/71

A run of cases finds the Tax Court refusing to find fraud in failure to file.

In the third case this month, the Tax Court has ruled against the IRS after it imposed the 50% penalty for fraud on a taxpayer who repeatedly failed to file.

The Tax Court recited in each instance that the burden of proof is on the IRS to show fraud by "clear and convincing" evidence. The latest decision involved a New York attorney who didn't file for four years.

The lawyer was "an intelligent, well-educated man" who met the tax obligations of his law practice (such as paying withholding taxes on time), but whose personal tax affairs were a mess. In eight earlier years he had filed returns late, though entirely voluntarily. His only excuse for failing to file was that he lacked the money, and his law practice kept him too busy. He meant to file and pay up eventually, he claimed.

The court decided that his intent to file late returns, as he had done before, "belies any fraudulent motive." It wasn't impressed by his excuses, but a "merely inadequate" explanation doesn't amount to fraud, it said.

(De Pumpo v. Commissioner, T.C. Memo. 1971-115.)
5/26/71

"The largest bootlegger in Harlan County" fares pretty well in the Tax Court.

Maggie Bailey, born in 1904, has been in the moonshine business since 1921, the court said. She neglected to pay income taxes until 1955 when a Federal agent called her attention to the oversight. In 1965 she was in tax trouble again when the Kentucky State Police found $207,000 in cash in her footlocker. That hoard contrasted with her style of life, which was partial to denim dresses or cast-off National Distillers Co. work clothes and tennis shoes.

The court counted the cash as unreported income over the years since 1941, but it refused to penalize her 50% for fraud. She kept no records, it conceded, but she did her business in cash and had no use for banks. The court had "more difficulty" comprehending the failure to file, but even that wasn't necessarily fraudulent.

The IRS never proved a specific sum was due in a specific year and fraudulently withheld, the court decided. But it held Miss Bailey liable for back taxes and late-filing penalties.

(Bailey v. Commissioner, T.C. Memo. 1970-64.)
4/1/70

In tax fraud, the burden of proof is on the IRS, and the Tax Court normally demands a clear showing that the IRS has met that test. The court recently declined to find fraud against a New Mexico man who ran a crap game and expanded into bookmaking. He falsified wagering tax returns, destroyed records and reported no bookmaking income. The IRS said that added up to fraudulent tax evasion, but he claimed he was just hiding from the police. The court had its doubts, but ruled the IRS didn't prove he was hiding income too.

(George v. Commissioner, T.C. Memo. 1970-231.)
8/19/70

An appeals court upholds a broker's conviction for willful failure to file.

Earl G. Baird conceded he hadn't filed returns for 1959 to 1963, when he made as much as $121,000 a year as a floor broker for Baird & Co., a firm headed by his brother, David G. Baird. But Earl Baird contended he wasn't criminally responsible because of mental disability. Two psychiatrists testified as to his incompetence. They were allowed to relate what Baird had told them in interviews, though normally this would have been excluded as hearsay. It was admitted solely to show what they had based their opinions on, even though it included Baird's saying he thought the returns were "taken care of" by a tax adviser.

The Government had Baird examined by its expert, who found him competent. That expert was also allowed to relate his out-of-court interview with Baird—

but no admission about the willfulness of not filing. Baird's counsel said the examination was self-incrimination because Baird had to submit and answer all questions. But the court ruled that having raised the plea and introduced his own experts, Baird couldn't object to the Government's.

The court also noted that, through the psychiatrists, Baird had got a favorable explanation on the record without submitting to cross-examination.

(Baird v. U.S.A., U.S. Ct. of Appeals, 2nd. Cir., 1969.)
9/10/69

A fraud penalty was overturned despite a taxpayer's questionable actions.

A Pennsylvanian didn't report his capital gain on a $160,000 stock sale in 1963. As part of the deal he had insisted on being paid with thirty-two $5,000 bills and given a receipt for only $120,000. He said he didn't want his estranged wife to know how much money he had. Later he deposited the bulk of the $5,000 bills in his checking account.

The man died in 1964. After the IRS discovered the stock sale, the taxpayer's estate paid the tax on the profit but balked at an added assessment for fraud. The Tax Court sided with the estate. Among other things, it noted that while the use of currency rather than a check in such a large deal might suggest fraud, the taxpayer's demand for $5,000 bills (there were only 555 in circulation) and his putting the money in his checking account were easily traceable actions that weren't consistent with the typical fraudulent intent to conceal.

The court said the taxpayer's conduct was suspicious and wasn't easily explained by his desire to deceive his wife. But it also held that suspicious behavior doesn't necessarily indicate fraud.

(Estate of Kauffman v. Commissioner, T.C. Memo. 1969-20.)
2/19/69

What Are a Taxpayer's Rights?

Another Circuit Court holds the IRS to its warnings policy on criminal cases.

The First Circuit has thrown out evidence collected by IRS special agents because they failed to follow rules the IRS announced in 1967 after the Supreme Court's Miranda decision. The IRS prescribed that when its special agents enter a case, they must warn the taxpayer their job is to look into criminal tax fraud. The special agents also must warn the taxpayer of his right to remain silent.

"Even though these standards may go somewhat further than the Constitution requires," the IRS must live up to what it said, the circuit court ruled. The policy was meant to foster "uniform conduct by all agents," but without court enforcement, there would be little incentive to comply. Further, the IRS made "a deliberate public announcement on which many taxpayers and their advisers could reasonably and expectably rely," the court said. After such a step, the IRS is bound by it.

"When an agency 'goes public' it does not do so lightly," the First Circuit said. The Fourth Circuit reached a similar conclusion late last year.

(U.S.A. v. Leahey, U.S. Ct. of Appeals, 1st Cir., 1970.)
10/21/70

The IRS' warnings policy in criminal cases can be flexible, a court says.

The IRS is supposed to warn a potential defendant of his right to remain silent when an investigation turns up evidence of criminal tax fraud. The tipoff usually is when an IRS "special" agent (they work only on criminal matters) takes over from a "revenue" agent. But one recent case showed there isn't a set way of deciding when the warning has to be given.

Having decided to start a criminal inquiry, a special agent accompanied a revenue agent to see the taxpayer. The revenue agent introduced the special agent only as "another man with the government." The agents asked for the man's records and he released them. Only later did the special agent identify himself and tell the man his rights. After he was indicted, the taxpayer claimed the special agent had tricked him into cooperating and tried to bar the evidence the agent obtained. But a circuit court admitted the evidence, ruling the special agent's reticence wasn't a "material misrepresentation" under the circumstances.

The taxpayer previously had loaned his records to the revenue agent for copying, and anything one gives the IRS voluntarily at the outset of a civil inquiry can be used later in a criminal action without his permission. Also, the man had disregarded his accountant's advice to stay silent.

(U.S.A. v. Bland, U.S. Ct. of Appeals, 5th Cir., 1972.)
4/19/72

Fifth Amendment rights apply in a civil case, an appeals court rules.

The Seventh Circuit decision apparently breaks new ground in extending traditional constitutional guarantees to civil proceedings. The case involved an IRS raid on a Chicago liquor store and bar, where bets were believed to be taken. The owner, who later said he was scared and nervous, talked freely with IRS agents. At no time was he warned of his rights to remain silent and get a lawyer.

The IRS conceded that failure to give the warnings barred use of the owner's statements in a criminal prosecution. But it used what he said as evidence in dunning him for underpayment of taxes and the 50% penalty for civil fraud. The Tax Court upheld that. The circuit court, however, found it "unwholesome and an abuse of power" to let the government base its civil case on an infringement of the man's constitutional protections. It ordered a new trial, with his statements excluded.

Barring the statements from the civil proceedings was a good way to deter the government from relying on improper procedures, the appeals court said.

(Romanelli v. Commissioner, U.S. Ct. of Appeals, 7th Cir., 1972.)
9/6/72

Seizing records from a taypayer violates the Fifth Amendment, a court says.

According to his employes, an Illinois doctor kept two sets of books—one of which was to be burned if the taxman ever came to the door. With affidavits to this effect, an IRS special agent obtained a search warrant and seized 35 cartons of records from the doctor's office and home. The doctor protested that the seizure violated constitutional guarantees against self-incrimination, and the Seventh Circuit appeals court readily agreed.

Even the IRS conceded that had it obtained a summons, it couldn't force the doctor to hand over his records. It contended, however, that its search warrant was valid, and thus the seizure didn't infringe on Fifth Amendment rights. That struck the court as "constitutional question begging." The IRS also argued that the doctor wasn't compelled to testify against himself. Other witnesses would have to establish that the records were authentic.

The court found "more shadow than substance" in

that distinction. A taxpayer's records "speak against him as clearly as his own voice," the court declared.

(Hill v. Philpott, U.S. Ct. of Appeals, 7th Cir., 1971.)
6/9/71

IRS access to a credit bureau's files is upheld over the firm's objections.

A recent circuit court case spotlighted a longstanding IRS practice of quietly tapping credit-bureau data banks for financial information about taxpayers. TRW Credit Data, whose files hold information on 20 million New Yorkers and Californians, contested the IRS right to compel it to give data on a taxpayer. The company demanded fair compensation, and it also asked a hearing on whether the IRS summons was burdensome or injurious.

"We question their right to such information in the first place," declares Gerald Davey, head of Credit Data. The circuit court disagreed. It ordered another hearing to set fair compensation (a lower court had said 75 cents a report), but it brushed aside Davey's substantive objections. "The Government has the right to require the production of information wherever it may be lodged . . . so long as it pays," the court said.

Industry sources say most credit companies cooperate with the IRS, sometimes under a summons issued on the spot. But in some instances, companies have refused and heard no more about it.

(U.S.A. v. Davey, U.S. Ct. of Appeals, 2nd Cir., 1970.)
6/13/70

Jersey Standard loses a legal test to close its board minutes to the IRS.

Auditing Standard Oil of New Jersey's consolidated tax return is a mammoth task, requiring the full-time work of four IRS agents. Since 1957, the IRS auditors have requested the minutes of meetings of directors and executive committees of Jersey Standard and many of its affiliates, including Humble Oil & Refining Co. Jersey complied for a decade, but in 1967 a new general counsel decided the IRS was asking more than the law allows. Instead, he offered to inform the IRS of top-level actions affecting the company's tax return.

A U.S. district court recently ruled, however, that Jersey must produce the minutes in full. The law allows the IRS to demand books and records that "may be relevant or material" to its purpose. The IRS can't be expected to take Jersey's word for what is relevant, the court said. Indeed, it noted, Jersey's accounting firm routinely requires full access to Jersey's files for its auditing.

Similarly, "IRS agents must inevitably look at things that are irrelevant and immaterial to avoid overlooking some that are relevant and material," the court said.

(U.S.A. v. Acker, U.S. Dist. Ct., So. Dist. New York, 1971.)
3/31/71

The IRS hones its scientific tools for tax detective work.

In the last year, IRS laboratory scientists have devised ways to check the authenticity of documents with unprecedented accuracy. By one test, called neutron activation analysis, the IRS can check the composition, age and origin of paper. The test sample is rendered radioactive in an atomic reactor, and the pattern of radioactivity is then examined. Another method, called thin-layer chromatography, determines the composition of inks.

The neutron activation was introduced several years ago to check the age of spirits being imported as brandies. Since then, it's often been used in moonshine cases. IRS officials say it's still rare to employ the complicated techniques in a special audit—they say maybe six or seven instances come up a year—but the ability is there.

3/4/70

State computers playback Federal tapes, confiding who tells the taxmen what.

Since 1935, Congress has authorized the IRS to tell state tax authorities what you put down on your Federal return. The states may pass on the data to localities. Now some 34 states get information on magnetic tape. Plugging the tapes into state computers can pinpoint which Federal taxpayers neglect to file state or local returns. It can also check the consistency of certain income figures. The IRS says it can't estimate what this information is worth to states, but state tax officials are enthusiastic.

"Our program would be crippled without this material," says Martin Huff, a California tax official. "It's worth millions of dollars"—in fiscal 1969, some $10.3 million in additional tax collections, he says. The Federal data are especially useful to California because the state doesn't require withholding of state income taxes. In Michigan, where an income tax was adopted in 1967, the Federal list of names and addresses was used to mail out tax returns. Currently, the state is gearing up to use the Federal tax data to make comparisons.

The IRS stresses that state and local officials who receive the information are bound by Federal restrictions on disclosure.

7/23/69

Trading tapes may be modern, but old-fashioned audits pay off, taxmen say.

Tax authorities always single out some returns for

close audits, and 44 states have agreed to exchange this audit information with the IRS. Generally, the audit sharing is "more productive" for states than uses made of the computer tapes, an official of the Federation of Tax Administrators says. "The first time around, matching lists of filers can be productive, but then the word gets out," he explains.

The audit information is worth $10 million a year to California, Mr. Huff estimates. New York State nets $10 million to $13 million annually by having its taxmen review audit changes ordered by Federal taxmen. (Taxpayers sometimes fail to tell state authorities when the IRS finds they owe more taxes than they originally declared.) In addition, New York says it has realized "tremendous savings" in manpower by splitting up audits with Federal taxmen and sharing the results.

7/23/69

What happens if your accountant discovers that through error, you materially underpaid your taxes in a previous year? According to the American Institute of Certified Public Accountants, a CPA must promptly notify a client if he turns up a material understatement. The CPA isn't ethically bound to tell the IRS, however, or even allowed to do so without his client's permission. If the client doesn't correct a material error, the institute says "the CPA will want to satisfy himself that (keeping the account) is compatible with . . . service to other taxpayers who assess themselves fairly."

10/14/70

The Swiss bank decision comes up with an important grant of authority.

Last December, the Swiss Federal Supreme Court upheld the right of Swiss authorities to give U.S. tax officials data from the "secret" bank account of a U.S. citizen under investigation for tax fraud. The full text of the decision, X v. The Federal Tax Administration, became available recently, and U.S. Treasury officials expressed delight with it. The decision interprets the U.S.-Swiss tax treaty, which authorizes the exchange of information necessary "for the prevention of fraud or the like."

The court brushed aside Swiss bank secrecy laws as inapplicable. In several cantons, it said, tax law provides that tax fraud be prosecuted under ordinary criminal procedure, and such procedure doesn't permit banks to withhold evidence in criminal investigations. The tax treaty extended this doctrine to all cantons, the court said. Otherwise, offenders could defeat the "spirit and purpose" of the treaty by switching their "fraudulent machinations" to cantons with laxer laws.

The Swiss insist their law has always provided for such disclosure, though they certainly haven't advertised it. They also note that under Swiss law, "simple tax evasion" isn't fraud.

(X v. The Federal Tax Administration, Swiss Federal Supreme Court, 1970.)
6/9/71

A five-year gap between indictments and trial isn't necessarily undue delay.

That's what the U.S. District Court for the Southern District of New York decided in ruling against a man indicted in 1965 on charges of helping to prepare a fraudulent tax return. The case had been adjourned a dozen times and then, in May 1966, removed from the court calendar at the government's request. Not until last February did the government indicate it was ready for trial.

The defendant claimed that was undue delay and asked to have the indictment dismissed. The district court reluctantly refused. Clearly the delay required an explanation, the court said, and the only explanation the government offered was inadvertence. But the defendant failed to show the delay had hurt his ability to rebut the government's case. (He had been at liberty the entire time.) Nor had he ever asked that the case be taken up.

Precedents in the Second Circuit left no ground to dismiss the indictment, the district court said. Failure to demand a speedy trial amounts to a waiver of the claim, the court recited.

(U.S.A. v. Schwartz, U.S. Dist. Ct., So. Dist. New York, 1971.)
5/26/71

Cough up: An accountant did a couple's tax returns for 11 years and routinely kept a copy for his files. There the copies rested until an IRS special agent called for an interview. The accountant put him off four days, then told him that regrettably, all copies and working papers had been returned to the couple two days earlier. A district court recently decided the papers remained the accountant's property, and the couple couldn't refuse to produce them.

(U.S.A. v. Widelski, U.S. Dist. Ct., East. Dist. Mich., 1970.)
11/11/70

No Fifth: A U.S. district court in California ordered an accountant to comply with a summons and produce working papers related to a corporate client's return. It wasn't impressed by a claim of Fifth Amendment protections against self-incrimination. It is "well settled law" that neither a corporation nor its officers or employes can invoke Fifth Amendment privilege with respect to corporate records.

(U.S.A. v. Machtinger, U.S. Dist. Ct., Central Dist. Calif., 1971)
6/30/71

A routine audit led the IRS to believe a banker had probably violated Federal law. The IRS wrote the Justice Department and told it so. At trial, the defendant claimed that initial letter was an unlawful disclosure of his tax return. But a U.S. district court in Connecticut said no. The letter gave nothing more specific than the man's name and address. (The IRS turned over its files later under authorized procedures.)

(U.S.A. v. Tucker, U.S. Dist. Ct., Dist. Com., 1970.)
9/9/70

Sacred trust: The IRS called in an attorney to ask about $12,000 in interest he allegedly paid a client who owed the Government taxes. The attorney replied that the client was in litigation, and any questions about the man were barred by the privilege covering dealings between lawyer and client. But a U.S. court of appeals was unimpressed. The IRS was merely looking for assets to get its tax money, it said. For the attorney to make a blanket claim of privilege "borders on the cavalier," the court declared.

(U.S.A. v. Finley, U.S. Ct. of Appeals, 5th Cir., 1970.)
11/25/70

An Illinois man charged the IRS with violating his civil rights by picking his return for audit, thus requiring more supporting data from him than from the millions who went unaudited. The Tax Court was baffled but unmoved.

5/13/70

Tax informants had a leaner year last year, the IRS says. Anyone who tells the tax men about someone else's tax evasion can claim a reward of up to 10% of the extra money collected. But in fiscal 1969, the IRS paid out $299,000 in rewards to 426 informants. That's off sharply from $403,000 collected by 462 informers the previous year and off even more from the year before that. In fiscal 1969, seven out of eight claims were turned down as unsubstantiated.

4/15/70

Tactics for the Taxpayer

"Silence is golden" in criminal tax fraud cases, a defense attorney says.

In the July issue of The Tax Adviser, Paul P. Lipton, a Milwaukee lawyer, argues "the advantages of non-cooperation." It's vital, he says, that rights be protected "from the earliest possible moment." The entry of an IRS special agent means the IRS has criminal charges in mind, but Constitutional rights may be claimed even earlier. The taxpayer should deal with the IRS only through his lawyer, he says.

The taxpayer can't be compelled to talk with IRS agents, Lipton advises, and "such interrogations seldom should be permitted (because they) invariably produce damaging admissions." Personal papers are also privileged, and "in most instances . . . it isn't advisable" to give them to the IRS. (On "rare occasions . . . full cooperation is proper.") The taxpayer should get his records back from his accountant, and it's "preferable" that the accountant (or others) talk to the IRS only under summons, with the taxpayer's lawyer present. Waiving the statute of limitations could mean giving away a good bargaining tool.

"Ironically, the cooperative taxpayer fares much worse," Lipton contends. "Tax prosecutions almost invariably are based in whole or large part on evidence furnished by cooperative taxpayers."

8/26/70

The IRS loses a tax dispute because it switched its ground in mid-argument.

If the IRS socks you for more taxes, it has to say why. That sounds simple enough, but in complicated tax litigation there's sometimes a temptation to slip from one issue to another. In one recent case, a Mississippi steel company bought a development company, but immediately sold off two chicken farms the subsidiary owned. It incurred a $227,257 loss. The IRS disputed the steel company's right to the deduction on the ground that it hadn't shown it acquired the subsidiary for a valid business purpose, rather than to take advantage of the loss.

At trial, lawyers for both sides agreed that was the only issue. But as things went along, the IRS abandoned that line of attack and seized on another possibility the taxpayer's lawyer alluded to. The steel concern couldn't take the deduction, the IRS then said, because the loss grew out of events before the merger.

The Tax Court refused to consider that argument, however. The IRS doesn't have to be consistent in what it argues, the court said, but it can't spring an issue it hasn't raised in its notice to the taxpayer or in its written pleadings.

(Mississippi Steel Corp. v. Commissioner, T.C. Memo. 1971-18.)
1/27/71

The Cohan rule helps a taxpayer who couldn't document his donation deductions.

Taxpayers who aren't as diligent about keeping records as they might be have long found some shelter in a precedent involving George M. Cohan, the composer. A tax tribunal had refused to allow Cohan any deduction at all for substantial business expenses because, it said, it was impossible to establish exactly how much he spent. Judge Learned Hand overruled that decision, however.

Complete certainty in such matters is usually impossible, Judge Hand said. If a court was satisfied that "something" was spent, it could make an estimate of what the minimum must have been. The court could of course "bear heavily" on a taxpayer whose "inexactitude is of his own making." In one recent Tax Court case, however, the taxpayer did pretty well under the Cohan rule. He had claimed $715 in charitable contributions, of which the IRS allowed only $15 for Christmas seals. The Tax Court restored an additional $625.

The Cohan rule doesn't apply to business deductions for travel, entertainment or gifts. Since 1962, the tax law has required detailed records of such outlays.

(Cohan v. Commissioner, U.S. Ct. of Appeals, 2nd Cir., 39 F. 2d 540.)
4/28/71

It sounds strange but a taxpayer can't use the figures the IRS uses against him.

A taxpayer was in a dispute with the IRS over how much support he had provided for his child, but he was willing to accept the IRS estimate of what his former wife contributed. The taxpayer had to prove he had put up more than she had. Apparently, he found it easier to take the IRS figures than to document his own version of the former wife's share.

The Tax Court, however, wouldn't accept the IRS agent's report as "competent evidence" of the former wife's share. The IRS based its conclusions on the report, but the taxpayer couldn't rely on it. For one thing, the court said, the IRS never claimed its estimate was complete. Once it decided her share topped his, it might well have stopped counting, the court surmised.

(Blanco v. Commissioner, 56 T.C. No. 39.)
6/23/71

Can taxpayers win access to IRS files? More than ever, a tax service maintains.

Since as early as 1888, the IRS has refused to divulge its official records, even in court proceedings. Now Tax Management Inc., an advisory group, contends there's a growing body of case law that enhances a taxpayer's access to private IRS papers if he's suing, or sued by, the Revenue Service. The group says that courts have granted access to IRS internal memoranda and official agents' manuals and also required IRS agents to give depositions.

In some cases, courts have granted access when the IRS assessed a tax deficiency without showing the basis for the assessment and it wasn't obvious. In other instances, Tax Management says, access was allowed when a taxpayer claimed that IRS action against him was based on an "improper purpose." Courts today are also less respectful of vague claims of "executive privilege" to justify secrecy.

In turn, a taxpayer must show a good reason for wanting access, the advisory service says. He can't be on a "fishing expedition" or using the request as a stall.

10/29/69

Now you see it, now you don't: The IRS has always resisted efforts to open its files to scrutiny. Recently, however, a U.S. district court ruled that two taxpayers the Revenue Service was suing were entitled to see and copy IRS regular and special agents' manuals and all material the IRS had obtained from the taxpayers. Four Revenuers were also required to give depositions. But the court ordered its order stayed pending an immediate appeal, because it saw "substantial ground for difference of opinion."

(U.S.A. v. Monsey, U.S. Dist. Ct., So. Dist. Ind., 1969.)
11/12/69

No peeking: When the IRS threw out almost all of the $16,000 in deductions a Chicago attorney claimed for business entertainment and gifts, he tried to subpoena the tax returns of 11 other law firms. The idea apparently was to show that such deductions were common, and his weren't out of line. But the Tax Court considered the other returns irrelevant. They wouldn't show that the lawyer kept the expense records required by law. Nor could the court assume that the deductions the others claimed were legitimate.

(Bane v. Commissioner, T.C. Memo. 1971-31.)
2/24/71

Turnabout: A California man filed suit in Federal court under the Freedom of Information Act on behalf of something called "Taxpayers Anonymous." He asked to do to the IRS what the law permits it to do to an individual taxpayer—"to examine (its) books and records." All he wanted was "a spot check," he said, "which shouldn't prove unduly burdensome." But the district court gave him short shrift. He hadn't exhausted his administrative remedies—gotten a definite "no" from the IRS—and he didn't specify the records he wanted.

(Abel v. I.R.S., U.S. Dist. Ct., Central Dist. Calif., 1970.)
9/23/70

A Few Shelters and Loopholes

The tax haven business is booming, says an Economist Intelligence Unit survey.

The research group, associated with The Economist, says developing countries are vying to give investors the most favorable tax deals. Most are tailored to the needs of the multinational company. According to the survey, the "artificial" holding company has probably become "a moribund tax avoidance device," thanks largely to loophole-plugging efforts by U.S. and British tax authorities. But havens abound for truly multinational firms.

"Every tax avoider is a special case and needs a particular kind of tax haven," says the survey, which profiles the dozen most prominent havens. The essentials are political stability, accessibility, and a low tax, or none, on at least one important income source. But while safe havens exist for firms or funds, "few people should flee to a tax haven purely to avoid tax," the survey advises. Higher living costs often wipe out any tax saving.

2/3/71

Tax loopholes? Here's a tax reform provision that comes personally engraved.

One part of the Tax Reform Act was widely known as tailored to benefit Station WWL, the CBS affiliate in New Orleans. The station belongs to Loyola University, a Jesuit institution. Senate Finance Committee Chairman Long pushed through an exemption for WWL from a tax on what religious groups earn from businesses unrelated to their religious functions.

The exemption is subject to three qualifications, which apparently only WWL can meet. A recent discovery makes that intent all too clear: In writing the law, the draftsman began each of the qualifying phrases so that together they spell out the station's call letters. Here's how it goes:

"Except . . . in the case of a trade or business . . .
"(A) Which consists of . . .
"(B) Which is carried on by . . .
"(C) Less than 10% of the net income . . ."

Capitol sources swear there was no coincidence.

5/27/70

Eureka? There's a hot new multipurpose tax shelter, a CPA firm advises.

It's called a tax-exempt bond. According to a Lybrand, Ross Bros. & Montgomery study, the combination of high interest rates and "tax reform" curbs on other devices has resurrected municipals and "moved (them) to the fore as investment vehicles." The Lybrand firm is advising its clients to consider tax-exempts in many cases where trusts are now used. These include supporting elderly parents, providing for a child's future needs, paying alimony and giving to charity.

For a 70% bracket investor, it would take $250,000 in 8% corporate bonds or $400,000 in stock paying 5% to match the $6,000 after-tax net of $100,000 in 6% tax-exempts. That's the nub of the matter, but Lybrand says tax-exempts may be worthwhile regardless of the bracket. And using tax-exempt income to support a relative, for example, avoids the legal costs of a trust, retains the relative as a dependent, and keeps control of the income-producing assets.

Inflation has favored equities over tax-exempts and other debt, but according to Lybrand's Jack Crestol, investors have found the stock market "is a two-way street."

5/13/70

The maximum tax on earned income "isn't the bonanza we expected," a lawyer says.

It was intended to wean executives and professionals away from complicated tax gimmicks by providing a lower top rate on earned income—60% in 1971 and 50% scheduled for 1972 and after. But V. Henry Rothschild II, speaking at a New York State bar association session, said his clients have found the tax saving isn't that great unless the taxpayer earns $100,000 or more. The ordinary marginal rate doesn't exceed 50% until the taxpayer makes about $60,000 (assuming a joint return and some deductions).

Other provisions may curb the advantage of the new ceiling, Rothschild said. The ceiling doesn't apply to deferred compensation, but if an executive takes all his pay currently, that may push whatever "non-earned" income he has into a higher bracket. Through another provision, the taxpayer with both earned and non-earned income loses part of his deductions. And more than $30,000 in "tax preference" income cuts use of the new ceiling rate.

2/3/71

The IRS gets a shearing when it tries to trim a Christmas-tree shelter.

Raising certain crops is a popular tax shelter because many costs are fully deductible as current business expenses while proceeds from the eventual sale of the crop are usually taxed at lower rates as a capital gain. The Tax Court recently rebuffed an IRS effort to tighten the loophole. A taxpayer owned a stand of Scotch pine trees, which he raised for sale as Christmas trees. The IRS refused his sizable deduction for fees he paid to have the trees sheared.

If Scotch pines aren't sheared annually, they lose their neat conical shape and their sales appeal. The taxmen contended that shearing converted the pines to a new and more valuable use as Christmas trees and was therefore a nondeductible capital expenditure. But the Tax Court ruled that, in practice, Scotch pines have only one use, and their marketability is the outcome of natural growth. The shearing was maintenance.

(Kinley v. Commissioner, 51 T.C. No. 102.)
4/2/69

The Treasury won't try to plug the new loophole in the minimum-tax provision.

"We have too many other higher priority items to make an issue over this," says one official. The change, passed in the closing days of the last Congress, modified the 10% minimum tax on certain "tax preference" income, and it will cost the Government about $100 million annually in revenues. The Treasury knew what was afoot, registered its opposition, but didn't—or couldn't—block the measure. It won't seek repeal this session.

Under the 1969 tax act, a 10% minimum tax has to be paid on "tax preference" income above $30,000, although that's offset by any Federal tax liabilities already paid. This was passed following publicity that 154 persons with gross incomes of $200,000 or more paid no Federal taxes in 1966. But the newly passed amendment allows a taxpayer to carry forward for seven years any Federal tax payment and thus offset the minimum tax on future tax-sheltered income.

1/13/71

Whatever happened to the 154 people who cleared $200,000 and paid no taxes?

For one thing, they multiplied. The 154 wealthy

"nontaxables" who served as horrible examples in debate over the Tax Reform Act were drawn from 1966 tax returns. In 1968, according to IRS figures, the number with adjusted gross incomes above $200,000 but no tax due jumped to 225. That includes 32 with more than $1 million and no tax, up from a mere 18 in 1966. All this was before the new act.

But Washington experts say it's tough to say how the new law will affect such rich nontaxables. They may switch their income into fields the new law didn't touch—municipal bonds, for example. They may tap deductions they didn't claim before. On request, the Treasury picked four returns from the 154 and estimated the tax that would be due when the new law comes fully into play (not until 1975). One person with $14.8 million would have to pay $4.8 million in taxes, rather than zero. But another with $860,000 would owe only $6,000.

Treasury officials say the 154 weren't the black hats they became in public debate. Many paid no tax because they gave heavily to charity. Worse—but less dramatic—inequities were found among taxpayers who paid taxes but very little.

6/17/70

Some special exceptions perish, others survive in the final version of the Tax Reform Act.

About two dozen exemptions—all couched in general terms but narrowly tailored to benefit one or two firms or organizations—were tucked into corners of the House and Senate versions of the law. Some were meant to spare a few foundations from a requirement that they get rid of "excess" holdings in a business. Most of these were dropped, Capitol sources say, because curbs in the final tax bill are much less severe than the original House plan. Thus special provisions for the Kellogg,

Olin, El Pomar and Benwood foundations were thrown out.

The law as enacted retained a tax break for Station WWL of New Orleans, owned by Jesuit Loyola University. But it dropped a similar benefit for Station WOI of Des Moines, owned by Iowa State. The law will allow Uniroyal Inc. an investment credit on a $73 million plant in Ardmore, Okla. A similar break for a $180 million Mobil Oil refinery died in conference committee. Lockheed Aircraft and McDonnell Douglas were also granted a partial stay on repeal of the investment credit, but a reprieve for Transamerica Corp. from new real estate rules was killed.

In a speech, Sen. Kennedy had scored the covertness—but not the merits—of the proposed exceptions. A tax break he endorsed for Western Massachusetts Electric Co. was dropped.

1/7/70

A tax haven for rich yacht owners weathers the tax reform storm.

William F. Buckley Jr. enjoys his two handsome yachts and hardly arches an eyebrow at the $50,000 a year it costs to operate them. To the contrary, the conservative writer figures the net cost of his boats at about $2,500 a year. Along with hundreds of other high-bracket yacht owners, Buckley cut his boating bill by going into the chartering business. You and five friends can charter his 60-foot Cyrano for about $55 per person a day.

Some yacht owners turn a profit from chartering, and all say they expect to do so. (Buckley even charges himself charter fees.) But yacht brokers say the main incentive is that "operating losses" can offset taxes on other income. According to Stanley Goldstein, a CPA in New York, one wealthy yacht owner had $50,000 in operating outlays plus $10,000 in depreciation. Charter income came to $20,000, leaving a $40,000 "loss." In his bracket, that saved $35,000 in taxes. His net cash outlay was only $30,000, so apart from depreciation, he turned a $5,000 profit.

Tax treatment of yacht chartering remains relatively straight-forward. The IRS simply says the charterer must "reasonably expect to ultimately make a profit."

3/25/70

One yacht owner went aground in the Tax Court when he claimed business losses.

In a recent case, the court refused to recognize a wealthy Californian's "losses" because he failed to show a bona fide intent to make money. The man owned two boats in turn, including a luxurious 70-footer originally built for a Spanish nobleman. He set up a business to produce coastal surveys and to charter his craft for pleasure or oceanographic work.

The Californian opened an office and bought some letterheads. He also spread the word that his boats were available for charter. He actually obtained some business—but not much. Of the 1,523 days he owned the nobleman's old yacht, it was used on business only 20 days. The court was more impressed by his personal use, which included living aboard for a year.

(McCormick v. Commissioner, T.C. Memo. 1969-261.)
3/25/70

Ireland offers a tax haven for artists to draw creative people to the Emerald Isle.

"It is a way to improve the quality of life in Ireland with little or no cost," a tax official says. "Tax-wise, we are losing next to nothing." Since April, the Irish Republic has offered a tax exemption for original, creative work in writing, musical composition, sculpture, painting and similar arts. Both Irishmen and foreigners may qualify as long as they live in Ireland.

If an artist isn't already recognized, he may submit a sample of his work to the Revenue Commission to determine its merit. The commission can consult an outside panel of experts, and the law is to be interpreted liberally, taxmen say. The exemption applies only to an artist's income from artistic pursuits.

Mervyn Wall, secretary of the Irish Arts Council, expects about 600 artists will benefit the first year. Tax officials say they have inquiries from about 20 foreign artists. "I don't think Picasso is going to move up here," says Mr. Wall, however. "An elderly man isn't going to move to a damp climate."

11/26/69

A baseball club can offer tax shelter, but who needs it? a Mets owner asks.

Tax lawyers say a wealthy backer can use a ball club's hefty start-up losses to offset taxes on other income. A later sale of the franchise is taxed as a capital gain. For this reason, several clubs are run as "subchapter S" corporations, which means they are taxed as partnerships. In addition, sport offers a rare chance to depreciate human beings—though this tax advantage has been reduced since the IRS ruled that the cost of acquiring players must be capitalized, not expensed.

Its first year or so, Metropolitan Baseball Club Inc. —that's the Mets—was a subchapter S corporation, G. H. Walker Jr., treasurer and part-owner, concedes. But the team didn't generate substantial tax losses. "We've had good fan support from the first," he says. The club won't divulge its income statement, but it has never paid a dividend, Mr. Walker says. "Everything's been plowed back to benefit baseball in New York."

The Orioles are among several publicly held ball

clubs. Some 203,600 shares of Baltimore Baseball Club Inc. are outstanding, with a floating supply of about 50,000 shares. Lewis & Stoehr Inc., which makes a market in the stock, says that at $19, despite the Series, it's underpriced.

10/22/69

Businesses may save on taxes by using appreciated property to pay dividends.

If a company has stock it bought for $10 but is currently worth $100, the firm can avoid taxes on the $90 appreciation by distributing the shares to stockholders as their dividend. In its newsletter, Lybrand, Ross Bros. & Montgomery, the CPA firm, says many of its business clients are doing this. Large, publicly held companies often use stock they acquired many years ago. Smaller, closely held firms often turn the trick with appreciated real estate.

For an individual shareholder, the fair market value of the property is his dividend. But if the shareholder is a corporation, it gets a real tax break, Lybrand says. Its taxable dividend is limited to the issuing company's cost basis—the $10 in this example—and the normal corporate 85% dividend credit would apply to that $10. This would leave a mere $1.50 taxable on the stock dividend worth $100, Lybrand says.

Previously, businesses often used appreciated property to re-acquire their own shares. Lybrand says. But a provision of the Tax Reform Act restricted that.

3/17/71

The IRS proves no dummy: It nails the owner of a wax museum for its taxes.

Back in 1962, a Canadian set up a wax-figure display at the Seattle World's Fair and dubbed it Tussaud's Wax Museums Inc., although records in the case don't show any connection with Madame Tussaud's in London. He leased wax dummies from their manufacturers for $20,000, and the display grossed better than $330,000 for its tax year 1963. But the Canadian tried to chop its tax bill through an intricate sale-and-leaseback plan. That called for setting up a Netherlands Antilles corporation to buy the dummies and lease them to Tussaud's for a hefty royalty. That corporation would be owned by a Bahamas corporation, wholly owned by the Canadian.

Last week, the Tax Court ruled that he "played a shell game" with Tussaud's assets. It held him responsible for $70,000 in taxes Tussaud's owed. (The court had already set aside the sale-and-leaseback as nonexistent and disallowed a $118,000 deduction for purported royalties.) The court said Tussaud's had in effect transferred property (about $183,000) to the Canadian for no economic consideration. This rendered Tussaud's insolvent and hindered or defrauded its creditor (the IRS).

Under Washington State law, this made the Canadian, as transferee, responsible for Tussaud's debts, the court said.

(Hicks v. Commissioner, T.C. Memo. 1970-267.)
10/7/70

A tax dodge to shave interest costs is closed down in Canada.

Canadian financial circles had worked out a routine by which nonresident lenders, mainly U.S. banks, could avoid Canada's 15% withholding tax on investment income. This in turn meant short-term borrowers in Canada could raise money at slightly lower costs by selling their paper to U.S. investors who went untaxed. Under the law, the U.S. investors could escape the withholding simply by selling the short-term paper back to a Canadian a day or so before the debt matured.

One provision of the sweeping tax legislation proposed by the Canadian government will block this routine for debt securities issued after June 18. The Financial Post estimates that the move will cause an outflow of at least $300 million in "nonresident" money. Dominion Securities Corp. Ltd. says short-term borrowers in Canada will face a "significantly reduced supply" of funds. Like many financial analysts, it expects short-term interest rates to increase.

6/30/71

In his dissent from the University Hill Foundation decision, Judge Schnacke dusted off a quotation from Judge Learned Hand that bears repeating every so often. To wit: "Any one may so arrange his affairs that his taxes shall be as low as possible; he is not bound to choose that pattern which will best pay the Treasury; there is not even a patriotic duty to increase one's taxes."

6/9/71

Tax reform's impact on corporate earnings and capital investment decisions will be "minimal," a study in the Financial Analysts Journal concludes. It surveyed how the new law would affect 35 corporations chosen at random from Fortune's 500. For the majority of large firms, the study concludes, phasing out the surtax will largely offset the loss of the investment tax credit and accelerated depreciation on real property. The law's bite will be "highly selective," with oil companies and certain capital-heavy firms clearly disadvantaged.

5/27/70

How the Foundations Fare

The Tax Reform Act, the ink hardly dry, undergoes a blue-ribbon critique.

The preliminary report of the Peterson commission on foundations and philanthropy has substantial, though low-keyed, criticisms of the new law. The group believes Congress fell into "a certain amount of overreaction," and at times voted new curbs on foundations on the basis of "anecdotal" data. It urges comprehensive auditing and stricter disclosure for foundations to give a better picture.

The commission found that grants to voter-registration drives made up "less than 0.1%" of all grants, and travel-study grants to individuals were "only a very tiny fraction." Yet Congressional concern over some Ford grants in these fields was in good part responsible for new restrictions on foundations. Similarly, the Peterson group said "both the critics and the panegyrists" are wrong if they think much foundation money goes into "political and social activism . . . at the 'cutting edge' of social change."

The commission stresses it agrees with much of the 1969 act, in particular with strict curbs on "self-dealing" and with requiring foundations to pay out a high percentage of their assets in annual grants.

5/13/70

The Treasury gets good marks from foundations in spelling out the Tax Reform Act.

"Thus far we've seen a real desire by the Treasury to make this law work," says David F. Freeman, president of the Council on Foundations. The new tax law subjects foundations to unprecedented regulation, but a year after it became law, foundation circles find relatively little to complain about in the Treasury's proposed regulations interpreting the act.

This isn't to say there aren't problems. Foundations are struggling with new record-keeping requirements, and small, understaffed foundations have found these especially vexing. Freeman estimates that the creation of new foundations has fallen off "very heavily" because of the new paper work and adverse tax treatment of gifts of appreciated property to foundations. And foundations are still perplexed over what prohibitions like the ban on "influencing legislation" will mean in practice.

An official at the Foundation Center thinks the Treasury has been too lenient in at least one respect—its interpretation of what foundations must disclose.

1/6/71

A new species of public document has been spawned by the Tax Reform Act.

May 17 was the deadline for foundations to file returns, and those with $5,000 in assets were also required to make public an annual report. Of late, major newspapers have been peppered with public notices offering "any citizen who requests it within 180 days" a chance to see the report of, for instance, the Association of Russian Cadets Graduated Outside of Russia.

Foundations aren't being flooded with requests. At Dillon, Read & Co., a startled secretary first suggested that a caller see August Belmont personally about his South Bay Fund (he was out of town), but then dug out the annual report. John F. Heimerdinger, a New Yorker, duly handed over his foundation's report, then asked warily whether the caller represented "a private interest or a government agency." At Hecht, Brayer & Grill, an accounting firm, a request for the Emanual Streisand Foundation report (Barbra Streisand's foundation) baffled everyone. The citizen was asked to call when Mr. Hecht was in.

Typically, a report lists stock as the foundation's assets and gifts to charities as its grants. Belmont's fund lists 46 gifts, the largest $1,000 and the smallest $7.50.

5/19/71

A Cleveland survey praises tax-exempt foundations.

Kent H. Smith, chairman emeritus of the Cleveland Foundation, commissioned a survey of schools, museums and welfare projects in Cleveland to determine the role of foundations in their funding. Of 127 groups that responded, 53% said their programs couldn't have started without foundation support. Some 28% said foundations provide their entire budget.

The survey concluded that foundations were the "only likely fund source" for many experimental efforts with little popular appeal. The ability of foundations to cut red tape and provide money quickly was also praised. Government grants were said to be scarce and laced with restrictions, while individuals rarely support basic research, some respondents said.

9/10/69

Community foundations expect to gain from curbs on private foundations.

Since the Tax Reform Act, "I haven't participated in setting up a single private foundation, and I wouldn't recommend one," says the top tax man at a first-rank CPA firm. But publicly supported community foundations are exempt from most of the act's restrictions. According to Herbert B. West, director of New York Community Trust, there's a definite aim to encourage people to leave their money to community foundations, rather than set up their own.

Mr. West describes a community foundation as a community endowment, benefiting a variety of local causes. His organization, for example, gave out $4.5 million last year from 240 different, earmarked funds. (One endows a cafeteria for those who "are hungry and without means.") The Cleveland Foundation, founded in 1914, is both the oldest and largest. In 1968, its assets came to $122 million. That year, there were 226 community foundations, the Council on Foundations says. It expects the new tax law to help generate more.

A benefactor can endow an earmarked fund under a New York Community Trust affiliate with as little as $5,000, Mr. West says.

4/1/70

Tax reform produces a headache for the Southern Regional Council.

The Tax Reform Act's stiff curbs on use of funds from tax-exempt foundations were supposedly tailored to spare the council, Dixie's largest and best-respected human relations agency. But the new law has had a sharp impact, mainly through a rule that an agency involved in voter registration can't get more than 25% of its support from one foundation. The Southern Regional Council gets much more than that from the Ford Foundation.

As a result, the council was forced to cut its ties to its Voter Education Project, through which it had funneled funds to build Negro voting strength in the South. The newly-separate voter project marked time for six months, awaiting a tax-exempt ruling. It made no grants in the first half of 1970, compared with 96 in the first five months of 1968, the last election year. In addition, this year the voter project must raise $500,000 on its own, and stay within the 25% rule.

The new law also requires far more stringent record-keeping and supervision of how funds are spent.

"We've got to remember to be prolific memo-writers to ourselves," says the council's Paul Anthony.

8/19/70

A gift to a foundation from a firm it owns is ruled a dividend.

Tax-exempt foundations are currently under fire in part because many have substantial business holdings. Critics contend such holdings are often managed with a greater eye to profit than to the foundation's charitable goals. They say, for example, that some foundations permit the firms they own to retain their earnings, rather than pay the dividends a normal business would be obliged to pay. A Treasury survey found that where foundations owned 50% or more of a firm, in two cases out of three, the stock had a zero yield.

Recently a U.S. circuit court ruled that a $100,000 payment to the Sid W. Richardson Foundation by the Richardson Carbon & Gasoline Co. was a dividend, rather than a tax-deductible gift. The foundation was willed 75% of the firm by the late Texas oilman. The remaining 25% was held by Percy R. Bass, Richardson's nephew and a director of the foundation.

"The conclusion is inescapable," the court said, "that any action (the firm) took was also an action taken by the persons who had sole control of the foundation."

(Richardson Carbon & Gasoline Co., U.S. Ct. of Appeals, 5th Cir., 1969.)
10/8/69

A court denies the University Hill Foundation its tax-exempt status.

The controversial foundation carried out an ingenious plan to raise money for Loyola University of Los Angeles. More than $10 million in taxes are at issue in the current litigation. Over nine years, the foundation bought 25 businesses, largely on credit, and promptly leased them back to their original owners. Subsequent profits went to the foundation as deductible payments of rent. The foundation then used that tax-free rental income to pay off the notes it gave to buy the businesses.

The foundation has donated about $2 million to Loyola and it has said it will give $4 million more if its tax-exempt status is upheld. The Tax Court ruled in its favor, but the Ninth Circuit appeals court recently reversed that decision. Clearly, it said, the foundation wasn't operated exclusively for charitable ends. It was "in the business of using its claimed tax exemption to buy used businesses," the court declared. It was "a used-business dealer."

Judge Schnacke dissented. The court was awed by the foundation's success, he said. It apparently saw "something sinister" in the "ingenious, complex and somewhat unorthodox" arrangements.

(University Hill Foundation v. Commissioner, U.S. Ct. of Appeals, 9th Cir., 1971.)
6/9/71

David G. Baird Sr., the New York financier, wins his long tax battle.

When his troubles began several years ago, Baird was senior trustee of the Winfield Baird Foundation. A congressional committee accused him of flagrantly misusing the foundation as a "multimillion-dollar tax-free securities dealer." And in one case, the Tax Court ruled that a $672,000 gift to the foundation was actually a taxable payment for Baird's alleged role in arranging a merger.

An appeals court rejected the ruling on the ground the IRS had broadened its original allegation without informing Baird. The IRS first said the payment was a finder's fee, then later claimed it also was payment for past and future services. The circuit court said Baird hadn't been given a fair chance to rebut the broader charge, so it returned the matter to the Tax Court and instructed it either to decide the case on the finder's fee theory alone or, if the IRS desired, to reopen the record for evidence on the expanded charge.

The IRS didn't ask for the record to be reopened, but simply maintained it had proved the finder's fee charge. The Tax Court disagreed, thus giving Baird the victory.

(Baird v. Commissioner, T.C. Memo. 1972-75.)
4/12/72

A foundation survived one challenge to its tax-exempt status but lost on another.

Its founder donated $1.2 million in "blue chip" securities in June 1960. A month later, the foundation bought $1,140,000 worth of stock in the founder's family corporation at $400 a share and paid for the stock out of the proceeds from the donated securities. The Tax Court held, and an appeals court agreed, that buying the stock from the donor's family didn't invalidate the foundation's exemption from Federal income taxes. The IRS had stipulated that the family corporation stock was worth $400 a share, the courts noted, and they decided the investment was sound for the foundation.

But the foundation ran into trouble in accumulating its income. Over a four-year period, it kept from 19.3% to 41.7% of its annual income, rather than distributing it in gifts. Since the foundation had no definite plan for using the money, the courts found the accumulations unreasonable and denied the exemption from taxes for the whole four years.

Private foundations generally face difficult times. Their tax exemptions are prime targets in current tax-reform efforts.

3/12/69

Some Tax-Exempt Groups

Social clubs face new guidelines on nonmember business, the IRS says.

The new requirements take effect July 1, 1971. They concern a perennial tax sorepoint, the use by nonmembers of facilities at tax-exempt country clubs, recreation centers and the like. Too much patronage from the general public may cost a club its exemption. Even if such use isn't excessive, the club may be liable for taxes on such income. The new IRS guidelines don't say flatly how much is too much, but generally if receipts from the general public are less than $2,500, or 5% of the club's total receipts, the exemption won't be in danger.

The "general public" includes anyone who isn't a member, a member's dependent, or his guest. The IRS says that a group of eight persons or fewer, including a member, will be assumed to be the member's guests, provided he or his employer pays. A similar assumption holds when 75% or more of a group are members, and a member or his employer pays. ("Adequate records" must document this.)

In all other instances involving nonmembers, the club must keep detailed records to IRS specifications, to substantiate the "host-guest" relationship.

(Rev. Procedure 71-17.)
5/19/71

A social club finds it can't use its losses to spare outside income from taxes.

The Adirondack League Club is a nonprofit social club that owns a 50,000-acre hunting and fishing reserve in the Adirondack Forest region. It lost its tax-exempt status years ago because it makes substantial income from timbering on its land. The league charges its members dues and fees for lodging and services, but it doesn't turn a profit on these operations.

The league was in the courts recently, and this time the question was whether it could use its losses on services to members to offset its taxable timbering income and thus escape taxes. The Tax Court ruled that it couldn't. The law provides a deduction for expenses incurred in carrying on a business, it said, but the services to members weren't part of the timbering business. In substance, the court said, the league distributed its timbering profits to its members in the form of lower dues and fees.

Congress didn't intend that a private social club, not taxable, subsidize its activities with outside income without paying taxes on that income, the court declared.

(Adirondack League Club v. Commissioner, 55 T.C. No. 83.)
3/3/71

Country clubs might raise dues, ban nonmembers in conforming to the tax act.

Before passage of the Tax Reform Act of 1969, most country and other social clubs were exempt from income taxes. Now clubs are required to pay taxes on income that isn't derived directly from providing services to members. Most income from investments and use of clubs by nonmembers, for example, is taxable beginning this year.

The Country Club of Ithaca in upstate New York might be "forced to curtail services for members' guests and raise dues," says its manager, Paul McGraw. A club in Washington State has similar fears. "A lot of economically marginal small clubs will go under (because of the law)," warns Jack Janetatos Jr., legal counsel to the National Club Association.

Many large, exclusive clubs claim the law's specific requirements aren't clear, but grumble the statute will complicate accounting and bookkeeping.

6/10/70

The IRS drops a rule that hospitals serve the poor free to qualify as tax-exempt.

For years it has said that a private, nonprofit hospital must be operated "to the extent of its financial ability for those not able to pay." Hospitals have opposed this, arguing in part that schools, museums and other causes aren't required to provide free programs. The hospitals also say that private and governmental medical insurance now covers most persons.

Last week the IRS ruled in effect that merely offering medical services to the general public is enough—provided a hospital isn't run by a small clique, or to benefit one, and no emergency patient is turned away. "We're delighted," the American Hospital Association delcares. Hospitals say they are glad to have their status clarified, but maintain that the ruling won't reduce the services given the poor. Joe Greathouse, administrator of Vanderbilt University Hospital, cites other factors—such as medical ethics, hospital charters, and licensing and accreditation requirements—that "strongly imply" a hospital must serve all segments of the community.

"The ruling won't affect what we do," says New York's Montefiore Hospital. "We've always considered ourselves a community hospital."

(Rev. Ruling 69-545.)
10/15/69

A "scientology" church is denied tax-exempt status: Better luck in the next life.

In a recent case, the Court of Claims ducked the

question of whether the cult is a legitimate church. Scientology teaches that each person contains an immortal spirit, which at death passes into another body. In the string of its lives, however, this spirit becomes inhibited by "engrams" or "detrimental aberrations," rising from misdeeds or unpleasant experiences. Scientology ministers claim they can ease the burden of these engrams by a certain "processing"—normally offered at $20 an hour for 25 hours.

The Court of Claims ruled that the Founding Church of Scientology, Washington, D.C., failed to prove it was entitled to tax-exempt status during the years at issue (1956, 1958 and 1959). It didn't show its net income didn't benefit private individuals. The court noted that the group had paid its founder more than $100,000 over four years, plus the use of a car and a home. His family had also received payments, some of them never explained. In some cases, the founder was also granted 10% of the gross income of affiliated Scientology havens. "Such an arrangement suggests a franchise network for private profit," the Claims Court declared.

(Founding Church of Scientology v. U.S., U.S. Ct. of Claims, 1969.)
7/30/69

More groups are considered exempt from Federal income taxes.

Among recent rulings, the Revenue Service held that a nonprofit organization formed to educate the public about an illegal activity and to seek legislation that would legalize the activity can qualify for exemption as a social welfare organization. The IRS said that even though the activity might be controversial, "the education of the public on such a subject is deemed beneficial to the community because society benefits from an informed citizenry."

Also ruled exempt is an organization formed for the multiple purposes of promoting racial integration in housing, lessening neighborhood tensions and preventing the deterioration of a neighborhood.

(Rev. Ruling 68-656 and Rev. Ruling 68-655.)
1/8/69

A Seventh Day Adventist couple claimed Social Security taxes abridged their religious freedom because they conscientiously objected to life insurance. The law does permit an exemption for adherents of a sect whose tenets forbid public or private insurance and which makes adequate provision for its members. But the Tax Court found it reasonable to limit the exemption to members of such sects. And the couple relied on the teachings of a prophet, not on a set position of their Church.

(Palmer v. Commissioner, 52 T.C. No. 36.)
6/4/69

A drug clinic qualifies as a tax-exempt charity, and thus donations to it are tax-deductible, the IRS rules. The ruling involved a nonprofit group that offers a 24-hour emergency rescue center to deal with bad trips on hallucinatory drugs. The group also gives out literature on drug hazards and sends speakers to local high schools.

(Rev. Ruling 70-590.)
12/2/70

A businessman's lunch isn't enough to warrant a tax exemption, the IRS rules. A club was organized as a gathering place for businessmen to talk over business affairs. It owned and operated luncheon and bar facilities, but that was as far as it went. And without a more substantial program, the group couldn't qualify as a tax-exempt business league.

(Rev. Ruling 70-244.)
5/27/70

Taxes Over the Long Haul

Where's "Charlie"? He's in a rut, with higher pay but soaring taxes and inflation.

The Tax Foundation sketched how "Charlie Green," an imaginary but typical white-collar worker, fared over the last decade. It found that earning $11,000, Charlie is no better off today than he was in 1960, when he made $7,500 a year. In 1960, total taxes took 23% of his pay. Today, it's 34%. And the rest of his salary increase has been eaten away by price inflation. His 1960 dollar has shrunk to 77 cents.

The foundation figures that Charlie's taxes more than doubled over the decade, jumping to $3,475 from $1,707. His state income tax bill is up 161%, and local taxes are up 108%. In 1960, Federal income taxes took 11% of his income; this year, they will run almost 14%. In fact, this year the Greens will spend 40% more on government than on food.

Charlie may get more in government services now than in 1960. But "we don't get into that," the foundation says.

8/19/70

When the GNP goes up 1%, federal revenues go up a comfortable 1.5%.

That's a key point in the Nixon version of revenue-sharing. By contrast, Rep. John B. Anderson, speaking for the administration, claims only 27% of state revenues come from high-growth levies. He says general sales tax yields barely keep pace with GNP growth, and property taxes go up only 0.7% for each 1% rise in GNP. Tobacco taxes (0.35%) and motor-fuel taxes (0.35%) are even more laggard.

Thus Rep. Anderson contends that a federal takeover of welfare outlays "attacks the wrong side of the ledger." It would relieve the states of a huge expenditure but do nothing to correct the "inherent inadequacy" of state and local revenue sources. Unless states and localities are plugged into the high-growth federal tax system, they face incessant needs to enact new taxes, Rep. Anderson argues.

2/17/71

Taxes and inflation eat up wage gains, a Teamsters study maintains.

New York City wage earners finished a poor third behind inflation and higher taxes in their actual claims on pay increases granted between 1964 and 1968, a study by Teamsters Joint Council No. 16 contends. In 12 industries, the study says, workers lost ground in the purchasing power of their take-home pay. Wholesale trade workers, for example, were given raises totaling $15.79 a week. But taxes took $7.51 and inflation $11.19, and the workers were $2.91 worse off.

It was the same story in union-bastion industries, the study says. Weekly pay of construction workers rose $30.43 to better than $201, but a tax bite of $13.21 and an inflation loss of $15.86 left a real gain of $1.36. "Collective bargaining by itself no longer enables the worker even to hold his own."

4/16/69

Invisible tax boosts continue as incomes edge upward into higher tax brackets.

As incomes rise, Uncle Sam not only has more income to tax but a bigger chunk of it comes under higher rates. According to newly released figures, the proportion of total returns with $10,000-or-more in adjusted gross income jumped better than 50% between 1965 and 1968. That's true even though three out of four returns still report less than $10,000. The proportion falling between $15,000 and $20,000 leaped 92% to one in 20.

To some extent Uncle Sam is benefiting from nominally higher incomes due to inflation. It's hard to say how much, but as a rough indication, Government figures show that per capita disposable income advanced 21% between 1965 and 1968. In 1958 dollars, however, the gain came to only 11%. Treasury people say the Tax Reform Act took some account of inflation when it liberalized personal exemptions and standard deductions.

But Treasury officials also contend the Government doesn't reap that much extra from the movement into higher brackets, whatever its cause. "The progressiveness of the tax system doesn't have that much bite," one official says.

3/20/70

Trust funds like Social Security grow ever larger, the Tax Foundation points out.

By year-end, federal trust funds will hold more than 25% of the public debt. In fiscal 1970, trust-fund outlays made up almost half of total federal spending for domestic purposes. During the 1960s, trust-fund receipts more than tripled, while general revenues rose only 88%. There are 831 separate funds, but 14 major trust funds account for almost all the total fund finances. They finance social insurance plans, federal employe pensions, veterans insurance and highway and airway improvements.

In theory, such funds are fed by user taxes or fees, but the Tax Foundation says they draw on "a substantial and increasing" amount of general revenues. As earmarked funds, they escape the normal appropriations process and introduce "a strong element of rigidity" in the budget. Their growth adds to "relatively uncontrollable" outlays in the budget.

They can also make federal finances look better. In 1969, there was a $3.2 billion surplus because an $8.7 billion trust-fund surplus more than offset a $5.5 billion deficit in other federal accounts.

2/10/71

Trouble looms for many state and local pension funds, the Tax Foundation warns.

In the last five years, the cost to taxpayers of the 2,100 pension systems covering non-Federal government employes has climbed 60% to $4 billion annually. The foundation sees no sign of a slowing. It looks for larger benefits, broader coverage and relatively smaller employe contributions. It expects the assets of all such funds to total $91 billion by 1975, compared with $43.6 billion at the end of 1968.

Many such systems are fiscally sound, the foundation says, but its survey found "numerous examples of serious underfunding." In some cases, government units have "no plans made for the day when the benefits due will exceed receipts. . . . Many systems may be in precisely this unrealistic and untenable condition," the foundation concludes.

4/8/70

Inflation has meant billions in extra business taxes, an accounting study says.

The study looks at the impact of inflation on the values assigned business inventories. It concludes that since World War II, business profits were overstated by $48.4 billion because of inflated inventories. This has meant $21.3 billion in additional taxes, including $6.1 billion in the last three years, it says. The study is in The Tax Adviser, published by the American Institute of Certified Public Accountants.

Inflation hits hard because firms determine costs by subtracting their closing inventory from their opening inventory (plus additions during the year). A higher closing figure means lower costs and thus higher profits and taxes. The accounting study suggests greater use of the LIFO inventory method—"last in, first out." LIFO assumes a firm is selling its newest stock. Thus items left on the shelf are assumed to be the oldest—and lowest valued.

The authors concede the LIFO method is more complicated. Yet they offer it as "an effective tool" to keep from overstating profits during inflation.

12/9/70

The consumer dollar, in terms of 1958, is worth only 75 cents now, but the purchasing power of a dollar in the hands of the government has slipped to a mere 61 cents, says Comptroller Arthur Levitt of New York State. That extra inflation bite comes because governments deal mainly in service, and their major purchases are things that have inflated the most: Wages and interest on debt. "The effect on taxpayers is tremendous," Levitt says.

12/16/70

Living wage? In Detroit, a teacher totted up his exemptions and deductions (less what he had paid in withholding) and came up with a figure of $8,770. He then claimed an additional "miscellaneous deduction" of $2,150 on his tax return. That, he explained in Tax Court, was the difference between the $8,770 he could deduct and the $10,920 the Bureau of Labor Statistics said was needed to support a family of four in "moderate" style. The court was unimpressed.

(Summers v. Commissioner, T.C. Memo. 1971-11.)
1/27/71

Brace yourself for "the long-term tax bind," Arthur Lipper Corp., New York, advises its investor clients. Over the long haul, it concludes, taxes at all levels aren't generating enough to pay for existing programs, much less proposed spending plans. "A significant portion" of economic growth may well go for higher taxes, rather than corporate or consumer spending. The impact on corporate profits "could be dramatic," Arthur Lipper says. At present, the part of U.S. GNP paid in taxes (29.4%) is lower than in any Western European nation except Switzerland, it adds.

7/15/70

Life Is Very Taxing These Days (III)

Calls from drunks are the least of Los Angeles tax authorities' problems.

Ever since mid-July, when the courts threw out the city's 5% tax on drinks served in bars, the tax refund office has been plagued with telephone calls from indignant inebriates. "They claim they're entitled to huge refunds," an official says. "From the way they sound, their claims are probably valid." But no refunds of the $10 million the city collected have been made, and no one yet knows what to do. "It's going to be difficult," sighs a deputy city attorney. A bill to allow the tax got nowhere in the state legislature.

Individuals, bar owners, liquor retailers, bar mitzvah hosts, and caterers have claimed more than $2 million in refunds. An "individual tippler" and two retailers have sued to force the city to put the $10 million in a trust fund. Los Angeles bars might tap that fund to buy people drinks, an attorney in the suit suggests.

That wouldn't give the money back to the people who paid the tax, he concedes. But it would achieve "a rough justice."

8/26/70

The Grass Is Always Greener?

Family tax burdens vary enormously from state to state, two studies show.

Most comparisons of the tax bite in different states are misleading because they include business tax collections or fail to allow for different income levels. Two recent sets of figures, however, relate the tax burden that actually weighs on various family incomes.

Recent Bureau of Labor Statistics figures show the personal taxes of $3,432 in metropolitan New York were almost twice the $1,767 in Austin, Texas. Both assume a family of four on a "higher" budget (U.S. average $14,-589) and 1968 tax rates. In Milwaukee, Boston, Minneapolis-St. Paul, and Buffalo, the tax share of the budget exceeded $3,000. In small Southern towns, Houston, Dallas, Nashville, and Orlando, it ran under $2,000. The U.S. average: $2,523.

Another study, also based on 1968 rates, of the bite of state and local taxes found it varied, but was solidly regressive in every state. On average, the state-local tax burden came to 12.8% of a $3,500 annual income, but only 5.4% of a $50,000 income. The study was by Professors Stephen Lile and Don Soule.

In Maine, Rhode Island, and New Jersey, the tax burden at the bottom of the ladder exceeded 16%, while in Washington State, Nevada, and Wyoming, the top-bracket bite was less than 3.5%.

3/4/70

Tax burdens vary widely among the 25 largest cities, a study of major taxes says.

In Milwaukee, a family of four with $10,000 in family income pays an estimated 15.9% in state and local taxes, the study says. That's four times the 4% "burden" in Houston and almost twice the 25-city average of 8.8%. The study was prepared by the District of Columbia government, and it covers sales, real property and non-Federal income levies. One finding: At $25,000 in family income, such taxes take 15.7% in Milwaukee, 13% in Baltimore and 12.1% in Boston—but only 3% in Houston, 3.2% in Dallas and 4.1% in Seattle.

In eight cities, the tax burden runs "much above the average," it says. These include Pittsburgh, Philadelphia, Indianapolis, New York and Phoenix, as well as top-levy Milwaukee, Baltimore and Boston. In nine of the 25 cities, tax systems are "progressive" (the rich pay a higher percentage), but in such cities, rates at all levels tend to run higher than average. Memphis, Seattle and New Orleans were found most "regressive"—the poor pay more. In Memphis, the extreme, a taxpayer with $5,000 in family income pays 8.3%, while someone with $25,000 is taxed only 5.7%.

There's great variation in real property taxes, the study finds—from more than 10% in Boston and Milwaukee to less than 3% in New Orleans and Houston.

12/16/70

An even trade is a rare exchange in the Federal budget's net impact on states.

In only 10 states does Federal spending roughly equal the Federal revenues raised within their borders. In 11 states, Federal outlays are substantially less and in the rest, substantially more, the National Industrial Conference Board finds in a study of where Uncle Sam collects and spends his money. Except for Minnesota, the seven industrial states touching on the Great Lakes glean 70 cents, or less, on the dollar. The profit-makers are the South, the Rocky Mountain and many Plains states, and unique areas like Alaska (which nets $4.50 on the tax dollar) and Hawaii ($2.30).

As a rule, higher-income states benefit less and poorer states more. But there are exceptions. Despite a decade of hand-wringing over West Virginia's plight, the state merely breaks even in the flow of funds. And because of its defense industry, well-off California reaps $1.30 in Federal outlays per tax dollar.

5/7/69

Americans pay lower income taxes than taxpayers in any Common Market country, the United Kingdom or Canada, a Towers, Perrin, Forster & Crosby study finds. An American making $30,000 in total pay is taxed at an effective rate of 22.4%, assuming a family of four and standard deductions. The Europeans pay from 23.4% in France to 51.3% in the Netherlands. (Four others are over 40%.) Only at $10,000 is France (10.2%) lower than the U.S. (11.2%). A Dutchman is dunned 28.9%.

6/24/70

Taxes in the South weigh heavily on the poor, the Southern Regional Council says.

"Southern states (1) have lower incomes, and (2) out of lower incomes, take a higher share in regressive taxes than the average state," concludes the Atlanta-based council, best known for its voter registration and civil rights work. In every Southern state except Texas and Virginia, the sales tax bite exceeds the national average of $32.08 per $1,000 of personal income. In Mississippi, the figure is $57.72, and the levy raises 78% of state tax receipts. (Sales taxes are usually termed regressive because the poor spend a larger part of their income on items taxed.)

The council finds the income tax "of major importance" only in Virginia and North Carolina. Southern states rely less on income taxes and levy them at less progressive rates, it says. Lacking other sources, many Southern localities are forced to depend heavily on user charges and fees.

The "outmoded tax structures" leave many Southern states unable to deal with "a host of unmet public needs," the council declares.

11/26/69

State tax increases may level off this year, as legislators prove resistant.

The record $4 billion round of new taxes enacted in 1969 may be exceeded, but not by much. Thus far this year, legislatures have put more than $1.5 billion in added taxes on the books. Tax matters are still up in the air in at least 10 states, however, with perhaps $2.5 billion in higher taxes at stake. The biggest lump is in Pennsylvania, where the new income tax, expected to raise $987 million, was ruled unconstitutional. A substitute proposal is due today or tomorrow.

Texas increased taxes $450 million, mainly by boosting its sales tax to 4% from 3.25%. New York expects $320 million more from a higher sales tax. Iowa raised taxes about 10%, mostly from stiffer income taxes. Connecticut is due for an individual income tax, expected to yield $350 million. But in Ohio, Gov. John Gilligan's proposal for net new taxes of $778 million is likely to be cut. Good-sized tax bites are still pending in Michigan, Massachusetts and Wisconsin.

Indiana Gov. Edgar D. Whitcomb vetoed a $748 million tax bundle and made the veto stick. California's Gov. Ronald Reagan chopped the legislature-approved budget by $504 million and claims no new taxes will be needed.

7/7/71

Populous states aren't the only ones to have their hassles over taxes.

California, New York and Pennsylvania have occupied center stage, but smaller states are having large-size troubles, too. In Nebraska, for example, a 30% increase in income taxes is considered certain, and it may run 40%. Gov. James Exon took office vowing to "veto, veto and veto" to hold the line. Veto he did (including a $50 million school aid bill), but taxes still must go up by $22 million in fiscal 1972 over $168 million in fiscal 1971.

The federal government has an important impact on Nebraska's tax squeeze. The state needs more money for welfare to meet federal standards. In addition, state income taxes are levied as a certain percentage of what individuals and businesses pay in federal income taxes. Nebraska expects that federal collections in the state will be lower next year because of higher personal deductions and more liberal business depreciation. The state would have to raise its rate just to stand still.

For 1971, the state tax was set at 10% of the federal tax due. It's expected that this fall Gov. Exon and the revenue commissioner will set a 13% rate for 1972.

7/21/71

The tax bite in the U.S. as a percentage of gross national product runs considerably lower than in Europe, the Tax Foundation finds. Using 1968 data, it figures that U.S. tax revenues at all levels come to 30% of GNP. That compares with 42% in Sweden, 37% in France, 35% in Germany and 34% in the United Kingdom. But elsewhere the percentage is still lower: Australia collects only 24%, Japan 19% and the Philippines 11%.

3/10/71

The Property Tax Under Fire

"The sad fact is almost nobody realizes how bad property tax assessments are."

That's the consensus of a panel of municipal, tax and planning experts. Property taxes yield more than $33 billion a year, but the panel sees the levy as too often assessed unevenly and haphazardly by undertrained and underpaid officials. The great disparities in assessment practices cause some cities to pass up as much as 50% of their potential take, the panel says. Most properties are assessed too low.

The panel also charges that too often the tax assessor is still a key fund-raiser in local politics. "The power structure" relies on large property owners, who expect low assessments in return. The panel asks that assessment rolls be publicized, and assessment appeals made easy. "Ninety per cent of today's homeowners mistakenly believe they are getting the best of a bad deal," it says.

Forty experts took part in the panel, sponsored by seven major civic groups along with the Schalkenbach Foundation and Time Inc. The report published in Nation's Cities, represents "broad and general agreement," though not unanimity.

5/20/70

Nader's new drive on unfair tax assessing spotlights a ripe target.

One hope is to extend his normal student following to enlist middle-class homeowners, who have a dollars-and-cents stake. Sam Simon, a Nader associate, says fair tax assessments could cut homeowners' tax burden by "as much as 25%." But a panel of 40 experts has concluded that homeowner attitudes are "one big reason" assessments are so uneven. People don't want equity, the panel said, but rather "inequity favorable to themselves."

In "too many thousands" of localities, the power structure depends for support on "big property owners" who expect bargain assessments in return, the panel said. It singled out assessments in New York State, Illinois, and Indiana as particularly bad. It called for greater disclosure of assessment negotiations, including the name of any law firm involved. "All too often . . . a few favored firms have a very profitable inside track," it said.

11/11/70

A Detroit suburb stirs debate on how hefty land taxes affected its boom.

Some urban scholars say American cities stifle new construction by taxing buildings too heavily and land too lightly. Recently, Southfield, Mich., has been praised as a sharp exception. By one account, the Detroit suburb became "the boomingest city in the state" after a 1962 survey doubled the assessment—and the taxes—on land, thereby permitting "a substantial reduction in the tax on improvements."

But local opinion is by no means unanimous. Former Mayor S. James Clarkson doesn't doubt the increased assessments were crucial. "If you tax land, you tax it into use," he declares. But others note that assessment at 50% of fair market value is set by Michigan's constitution. They cite other reasons for the city's growth. "Probably most important," says Mayor Norman W. Feder, was a network of expressways that eases access to the city. Another allure was the huge Northland shopping center. And Southfield lies in the path of expansion from Detroit.

"The tax philosophy played no constructive part," one large property owner contends. The heavier land assessments "prevented or delayed improvements we otherwise would have carried out."

4/23/69

A ceiling on property taxes is proposed by an intergovernmental group.

The Advisory Commission on Intergovernmental Relations estimates that the average U.S. urban family pays about 4% of its household income in local property taxes, either directly or in its rent. Yet about three million households pay 10% or more—"a truly extraordinary tax burden," the commission says. In 1968, Wisconsin granted tax relief to 66,000 low-income elderly. For 22,000 of these people, their property tax would otherwise have taken 20% of family income and often much more.

With state legislatures in session, the commission has revived its proposal for a "circuit-breaker" provision that would in effect refund property taxes above a certain percentage of income. Four states—Wisconsin, Minnesota, Vermont and Kansas—have such laws. All four plans are limited to the low-income elderly. In Wisconsin, when such a taxpayer's property tax exceeds about 11% of his income, he gets a tax credit or a cash refund of the difference, within certain limits, the commission says.

The elderly are the neediest, but the commission recommends that circuit-breakers apply to all low-income families.

3/17/71

Wisconsin helps more low-income elderly persons with local property taxes.

The state offsets part of the property tax bite by giving income tax credits or cash refunds to persons 65 or older whose household incomes are under $3,500. An old person or couple who pays $250 in local property taxes can expect a $23.70 refund from the state if household income was $2,900, and a $122.70 refund if income was $1,500. Renters as well as homeowners are included: 25% of rent is considered payment of taxes.

A Federal advisory commission lauds the Wisconsin program as effective relief without an unreasonable drain on the state treasury. In fiscal 67-68, some 68,400 elderly claimants got an average of about $90 each. In the fiscal year beginning this July 1, it's expected that claims will grow to 78,300 and average payments to $97.50. Some tax people believe that extending the benefits to all low-income groups is a logical next step.

2/19/69

More states enact property tax relief, usually limited to the elderly.

Florida increased its homestead exemption to $10,000 for taxpayers 65 or older. South Carolina passed a homestead exemption for the elderly that's expected to cost $1.5 million next year. Colorado has granted an income tax credit or refund of up to $200 for part of property taxes paid. It's restricted to the elderly with net worth less than $20,000 and with income less than $3,700 if married.

Iowa and Vermont also passed measures for the elderly, but not all relief is for old folks only. Oregon enacted $20 million in tax relief for homestead owners. It comes into play when property taxes exceed a certain percentage of household income (3% for incomes under $1,500, with relief limited to $400 in that bracket). In Washington State, tax relief includes a provision that will reduce property taxes by $43.9 million in the next two years. It requires counties, when revaluing properties, to reduce assessment ratios to the average county ratio.

In Ohio, some sort of across-the-board property tax relief is considered likely. Gov. John Gilligan has proposed a rollback of $111 million in school taxes and $12 million in county welfare taxes, but the legislature may have its own ideas.

7/14/71

School and welfare tax burdens should be radically reshuffled, a panel says.

That's the proposal of the Advisory Commission on Intergovernmental Relations, which includes key officials from the Administration, Congress and states and localities. The states should take over "substantially all" the financing—but not the control—of local schools, the commission recommends. This would free about half of local property tax revenues for such other city duties as police and sanitation. "The consequences of low quality," the report says, "are felt far beyond the borders of an individual school district."

It also urges "full Federal financing" of welfare, which would spare state and local governments about $4.6 billion of annual outlays and almost double the Federal Government's $5.2 billion share. States and cities "have no real control over the root causes of poverty" or even over how welfare programs are run (because of Federal rules), the commission's executive director contends.

Five of the 26 panel members dissented, but Budget Director Mayo, Housing Secretary Romney and HEW Secretary Finch were listed with the majority.

12/3/69

Lowering the age required for voting to 18 may give bond issues a boost.

Many analysts expect the newly eligible young people to be more receptive to government projects and less concerned with property tax increases. "That's the only way I can see it going," says John Petersen of the Investment Bankers Association. About 11 million persons are in the 18-to-20 age group.

Traditionally, many young people don't turn out to vote, but Petersen considers it entirely possible to mobilize their support for bond issues. In particular, young people should back debt issues to pay for environmental or antipollution programs, a rapidly growing segment of the bond market. Many bond votes are close, and "a swing of five percentage points can be pretty damned important," Petersen says.

7/21/71

Property taxes are presumably a tax on wealth, but according to a Rand Corp. study of rental housing in New York City, they amount to a 30% tax on consumption of rented shelter. City taxes on real estate add "roughly one-third" to the typical family's rent bill, the study says. It also found that the effective tax rate on market value runs about 30% higher on multiple-family buildings than on one-family and two-family housing.

8/12/70

Rule of thumb—or of thumbs down? Whenever a school district's property tax hits 4% of true market value, you can expect trouble from homeowners. That's the experience of Engelhardt & Engelhardt Inc., a consulting firm that advises school districts on financing. The 4% threshold triggers protests, organized debates and other controversy, the firm says.

12/23/70

Old soldiers: Effective Sept. 9, Oregon will no longer allow a property tax exemption for disabled veterans of the Mexican War, Civil War or Indian Wars.

7/14/71

Taxes as Carrot or Stick

Tax credits as a carrot are an uncertain instrument, a foundation study concludes.

Ever since Alexander Hamilton proposed protective tariffs, Federal tax policy has had more in mind than raising money. Dangling a tax break as a reward has been a typically American approach to tackling social goals. The Treasury has estimated that currently the Government "spends" about $40 billion annually through tax preferences—that is, its possible collections are lower by that amount. And the Administration has indicated it hopes to use tax credits to mobilize private industry against a broad range of social ills.

But tax credits are by no means "simple, automatic, self-enforcing solutions," the Tax Foundation warns. "Great uncertainty" exists in judging how well credits work. For one thing, a credit may simply prove a windfall for things taxpayers would do anyway. For another, credits alone can't solve the difficulties inherent in thorny social problems. Tax credits, the foundation says, are usually less important than routine factors shaping business decisions—such as markets, labor, and materials.

Proponents of credits say they create less red tape and leave more elbow room than direct government outlays. That may be true, the foundation says, but it may also hide the true costs of tax credits.

2/11/70

A tax prod for New York City cigaret smokers may be filtered out.

Mayor Lindsay's tax planners dolled up the July 1

cigaret tax increase as a "good" tax by pegging it to tar and nicotine levels. Taxes went up four cents a pack on cigarets with more than 17 milligrams of tar and more than 1.1 milligrams of nicotine. If a brand flunked one test, but not the other, the added tax was three cents. No increase applied to cigarets low in both tar and nicotine.

Many retailers simply bumped all brands a nickel higher, however, and New Yorkers are "calling up like mad" to complain, city tax authorities say. More than 30 brands or variations qualify for no increase. (They carry orange tax stamps.) City tax people say they're concerned, but unless a seller misrepresents the amount going for taxes, there's apparently nothing the city can do. "Let the buyer beware," a city spokesman says.

7/7/71

Do tax levels influence where new plants are located? Probably not, a study says.

Many economists have concluded that tax differences among various regions have had scant influence in drawing new industry. Factors like labor costs and nearness to materials and markets have been found much more important. Now a study concludes that even in a local area, sharply differing tax levels have virtually no impact. The study by Helene A. Cameron, an Ohio State professor, was published in (Tax) Assessors News Letter.

The Cameron study relied on property tax levels in Franklin County (Columbus), Ohio. These ranged from $27 per $1,000 of assessed valuation to $51 per $1,000. Prof. Cameron used tax and business data to sketch several hypothetical concerns. She then found that the difference for these companies between paying the county's highest taxes and paying its lowest amounted to a mere 1% of operating costs, or even less. It was unlikely, she concluded, that businesses could or would base the choice of plant sites on so small a difference.

Plants tended to cluster in low-tax areas, she said, but taxes were low because many plants were there (for other reasons), and not vice versa.

12/3/69

Small-town tax coffers rarely gain when industry comes to town, a study suggests.

A new factory may bring sorely needed jobs and boost local businesses, but it will probably cost local governments more for additional services than it provides in higher tax receipts. That's the findings of a study for the Agriculture Department of five little towns in Kentucky. All five rural areas were heavily dependent on farming, low in income, and afflicted with serious underemployment.

The study compared tax receipts before and after a new industry came to town. In almost every case, the increased revenues failed to cover the cost of additional services. The short-fall was generally small, however, with the largest only $3,400 a year. The factories usually hired local people, but even a moderate influx of new families saddled the school district with more new expenses than new revenues. Another negative factor was tax concessions—various forms of relief from local property taxes.

The study tried to gauge the indirect effects of industry by comparing similar towns that lacked industry. It found no evidence that industry indirectly affected either tax receipts or expenditures.

10/7/70

A Louisiana program to attract industry draws some controversy as well.

Thus far this year, the state has exempted almost

$400 million in new or expanded manufacturing facilities from state and local ad valorem taxes. The 10-year exemptions generally amount to about 1% of a plant's total value a year. "This thing has worked out very well," a state official says. In the next five years, at least $250 million a year should be added to tax rolls as past exemptions expire, he says. After that, the rate should double, he predicts.

But not everyone believes the concessions lure much industry that wouldn't come anyway. "They're not as effective as better government would be," says the Public Affairs Research Council, a watchdog group. A Council official says that the exempted plants can severely strain localities by requiring public services without making an offsetting contribution to tax receipts.

Stauffer Chemical Co. received the largest recent exemption, for a $32 million chlorine-caustic plant. The company says "a composite of many factors" determined its site choice, including the tax concessions and a big customer nearby.

8/6/69

A businessman advocates tax credits as one way to resurrect the ghetto economy.

Theodore L. Cross, a financial executive, regards the wealth-creating techniques of private business as vital in any attack on ghetto poverty. But he argues in a new book, "Black Capitalism: A Strategy for Business in the Ghetto," that white business efforts in the black ghettos will sorely lack staying power as long as they are rooted in "corporate citizenship" or anti-riot palliatives. Cross would tailor tax incentives and loan guarantees to make it profitable for investors to bring venture capital, time and talent into the ghettos.

Cross bases his ideas on a hard-headed analysis of the black ghetto as an economic wasteland—"an economy that abolished wealth." He describes the ghetto as isolated from the main economy, unproductive and bereft of purchasing power. Entrepreneurial skills are rare. In the ghetto, Cross maintains day-to-day entanglements crush profit-making ventures. Routine credit doesn't exist except on loan-shark terms, he says, and savings and other sources of risk-taking "front-end money" are practically non-existent.

8/27/69

An incentive to work can be costly, a study of a negative income tax finds.

It's easy enough to bring 6.7 million poor families up to the Federally defined poverty line ($3,130 for a family of four). Direct payments totaling $15.5 billion annually would do the trick, a study sponsored by the American Bar Foundation says. But flat payments leave recipients no incentive to work, the study notes. Earning an extra dollar merely cuts the payment by a like amount, so why bother?

Surprisingly, the study finds it could be much more costly to devise a negative income tax that doesn't stifle an urge to earn more. One such plan would tax total family income at a flat 50%, but then subtract from a family's tax bill a "basic allowance." If the allowance exceeded the taxes due, the family would get Uncle Sam's check for the difference. Thus if a family earned an extra dollar, it would keep 50 cents, and taxes would take the other 50 cents.

But if the basic allowance were set at the poverty line, the negative income tax would cost $40 billion a year, the study expects. It's high because every low-income family, regardless of its earnings, gets the full allowance. The earnings in turn are only partly captured by taxes.

6/11/69

Bargain 'loans': New York moves to thwart borrowing by skipping taxes.

The finance committee of its city council yesterday favorably reported a bill raising the penalty on past due real estate taxes to 12% from 7%. Passage soon is considered almost certain. In April, the city had some $121 million in back property taxes on its books. The city claims that many real estate operators, including some of New York's largest property owners, find it cheaper to withhold their taxes and absorb the penalty, rather than borrow at today's peak rates.

"They hold out for four years and then kick in just before a lien is smacked on their property," a city finance official says. The city raised the penalty about a year ago, he continues, but money rates have risen still higher. "Our feeling is that 12% is about the minimum," he says. "We've got to make it completely untenable for these guys to hold out."

Mayor Lindsay backs the bill, and it enjoys bipartisan council support.

6/25/69

The Cities' Tax Plight

Do cities subsidize their suburbs? Yes, indeed, if Detroit is any example.

The 1970 census will show surging growth in the suburbs. That gives new bite to the old question of whether suburbs enjoy city services they don't pay for. Detroit, for one, clearly comes out short in the exchange with its suburbs, according to a study by Prof. William Neenan of Michigan, published in the National Tax Journal.

The study makes separate estimates for six suburbs of how much use their residents make of Detroit facilities. It covers libraries, parks, streets, university, hospitals and low-cost water supply. It also allows for the city's heavier outlays on poverty. In turn, these costs are offset by what each suburb contributes to Detroit through various state taxes, the city's non-resident tax, and other ways.

Neenan finds that in 1966, Roseville, a modest-income, residential suburb, used facilities that cost Detroit $10.56 per capita, but "paid" $3.32 in return, for a $7.24 "subsidy." Dearborn, middle-income and industrial, got $6.90 and paid $2.53. Allen Park, middle-income and residential, used $6.66 and paid $3.34.

Among the six, only high-income, residential Grosse Point Park paid more ($9.75) than Detroit's outlays ($7.91).

9/2/70

The Detroit data indicate that suburbs could be taxed more heavily for city services.

Except in one case, Detroit recovers less than its

costs for services it provides its suburbs. But Prof. Neenan's study has an interesting twist: In the private economy, an item is worth to an individual what he chooses to pay for it. But what is a park, or a zoo, or a poverty program, worth to taxpayers? Prof. Neenan figures that the higher a person's income, the more willing he usually is to support programs that don't benefit him directly.

On this basis, he concludes that high-income suburbs like Birmingham would be willing to pay as much as $18.22 for services it cost Detroit $9.02 to provide. (Birmingham actually paid $5.64, according to the study.) This means, Prof. Neenan says, that the suburbs' tax contribution to the central city could be "markedly increased" before the suburbanites would likely feel they weren't getting their money's worth.

9/2/70

Cities could squeeze much more revenue from user fees, the Tax Foundation says.

User charges, from library fines to greens fees at city golf courses, currently run almost $2.5 billion and make up about 16% of municipal revenues, the foundation says. In recent years, city outlays have grown almost 40% faster than general revenues, and user fees have been vital in helping to bridge the gap. Cities under 500,000 have made more use of such fees, while larger cities turn more readily to sales and income taxes.

There's still good potential for more money from fees, the foundation says. It names home garbage collection, sewerage, water supply, parking and building inspection as "logical areas" where full costs can be charged to users. But service charges are suitable wherever services benefit particular individuals without general social benefits (such as those from education), and substantial waste of the service would result without a fee.

In some cases—like free medical care for the indigent—charges would violate other norms. But special provision can be made, the study says.

10/7/70

"Local income taxes appear far more likely to spread than to wither away."

So says a study by the Advisory Commission on Intergovernmental Relations, a blue-ribbon group. According to the study, more than 3,500 local jurisdictions already have income taxes. That includes 49 cities of 50,000 or more. A revenue pinch gives obvious impetus to local levies. They also relieve pressure on over-taxed property bases. Even with flat rates, the local income taxes are usually less regressive than property taxes.

Surprisingly, the commission's study declares there's really "no compelling case" for graduated income tax rates at the local level. Though rates are flat, they tend to be low. A progressive rate structure would complicate administration of local income levies. And more basic, the study says, progressive rates are essentially meant to redistribute income. Localities, with their limited reach, are ill equipped to do this, it declares.

Taxing commuters as well as residents has become the rule, the study says. It's estimated that Washington, D.C.—still an exception to that rule—could pick up $40 million a year by taxing commuters.

7/8/70

Center City residents commonly pay much higher taxes than their suburban neighbors, a new report from the Advisory Commission on Intergovernmental Relations confirms. Its study of 37 metropolitan areas found center-city taxes averaged $219 per capita, while the suburban average was $170. But school taxes are often higher in the suburbs. They averaged $96 per capita, compared with $73 in the cities.

2/25/70

Sales tax credits against income taxes are popular, but can be oversold.

So concludes Elsie M. Watters, who directs state and local research for the Tax Foundation. By most tests, the sales tax stands up "quite favorably," she writes. It pumps out a lot of revenue, at rates low enough to minimize economic dislocation. The tax is stable, broad-based, easy to administer, and has potential for steady growth. The trouble is, it has a bad name as "regressive"—falling more heavily on the poor.

States have tried to spruce up the tax's image by exempting food purchases or giving a tax credit against income taxes. Fifteen states currently exempt food, seven grant a credit, and three do both. The tax credit is more popular now, but it isn't above criticism. Some say it erodes the tax base too much. Others question whether it really helps the poor. Often the poor don't know how to claim the credit, critics say.

"A mild note" of further caution should be sounded, Miss Watters writes. Proponents exaggerate the credit's impact. "A minidose of tax relief" isn't going to solve deep-rooted problems like poverty.

9/9/70

Commuting to New York from Fairfield County, Conn., cuts take-home pay by as much as 12%, according to Pitney-Bowes Inc., headquartered in Stamford. A Fairfield County man who makes $18,000 and works near home nets $14,926 after taxes, the firm says. A commuter earning $18,000 has $14,013 left after Federal, New York State, and New York City taxes. Station parking, commutation and subways cut that to $13,292.

2/18/70

Success story: Twenty-five years ago, only New York and New Orleans had a city sales tax. Today, according to the Tax Foundation, more than 3,500 local governments have adopted the levy, as well as 44 states. About one city in six has a sales tax, including at least half the cities of 300,000 or more. The sales tax is the top revenue source in 34 states. Eight rely on it for 40% of their taxes.

11/11/70

Gambling: The 'Painless' Tax

Is sin the salvation? Some states look to gambling as their tax plight tightens.

None of the existing lotteries has had a major impact on state finances, but cash-shy states are apparently willing to take a chance. Connecticut is sorely strapped for money, and Gov. Thomas Meskill has already budgeted $2.5 million from a lottery that doesn't yet exist. A lottery never really worked in New Hampshire, but there's a move afoot there to legalize casino gambling at local option. A casino proposal in New York is counted dead, at least for this year.

In Maryland, Massachusetts and California, off-track betting is getting various degrees of serious attention. In normally straight-laced Virginia, the General Assembly has authorized a commission to look into pari-mutuel horse racing. Pennsylvania Gov. Milton Shapp says he favors a lottery, but isn't really pushing it. In California, there's a lottery proposal—along with the usual bill to legalize jai-alai—but neither is given much chance.

Backers claim that legal casinos in Atlantic City would earn $200 million a year for New Jersey. Assuming tax rates used in Nevada, that would require an annual "handle" of no less than $80 billion in bets, an official estimates.

3/3/71

New Jersey is an oddity among lottery states: Its take is better than predicted.

The first eight weekly drawings averaged about 5.6 million tickets sold, more than three times expectations.

Backers credit the 50-cent ticket and its wide availability. It was originally predicted that the lottery would net $7.5 million for schools. Now backers are gleefully upping the estimate to as much as $30 million. But that's still toward an overall state budget of more than $1 billion.

Across the Hudson in New York, the lottery has earned only $110.9 million for education in its 44-month history. But the state's results jumped sharply last year when it introduced $1 million prizes and experimented with 50-cent tickets. In New Hampshire, the lottery has netted a disappointing $10.7 million for education in seven years. Its $900,000 net in 1970 was about 8% of the state's share of school costs.

3/3/71

While some states talk about legalizing gambling, Nevada just counts its chips.

Currently "the only game in town," Nevada relies on gambling for 70% of its economic base, officials estimate. About 45% of the state's general fund revenue comes directly from taxes on gambling, and officials say another 25% is collected from tourists paying taxes on clothing, food and gas. Nevada taxes on the casinos' gross has climbed steadily to $39.3 million in fiscal 1970 from $18.8 million four years earlier.

Officials say that gambling is almost recession-proof, but in recent months the state's take has shown some softening. The state has grown accustomed to a 17% annual growth rate, but currently the growth is running 9% to 10%. Nevada officials say they aren't worried about state lotteries, off-track betting or horse-racing elsewhere. They are concerned, however, about casino gambling proposed in other states—such as for Atlantic City, N.J.

One New Jersey official has his doubts, however. He

suggests that well-heeled Eastern high-rollers would still flock to Las Vegas. Atlantic City would get "anybody who can afford bus fare from Philly," he says.

3/10/71

Montreal loses a legal fight to keep its "voluntary tax assessment" alive.

The plan was begun in May 1968, but four months later it was ruled an illegal lottery by a Quebec court. The Superior Court of Canada recently affirmed that decision. Under the scheme, persons anywhere in the world could pay a $2 "tax" for a chance to win as much as $100,000 in a monthly drawing. (One winner was from Laos.) The city had expected to average $3 million in monthly receipts, but in the 19 months the plan lasted, only $17.1 million was paid in. About $3.5 million was awarded in prizes, and Montreal netted $10 million.

To get around legal restrictions, the city paid prizes in silver ingots instead of cash and required winners to answer factual questions about Montreal. Conveniently, however, rare metal dealers were always on hand to buy the ingots, and the questions came from 20 facts printed on contestants' receipts.

Only one person whose name was drawn (for a $1,000 prize) ever flubbed the "skill-testing" poser. The city's 40 city councillors passed the hat and gave him $1,000 anyway.

1/7/70

That lottery in New York State with the $1 million first prize topped all expectations. Tax officials were delighted when sales of the $3 tickets seemed certain to exceed $10 million. Now they are bowled over by final figures that show better than $16.7 million in receipts. The law specifies that 40% must be paid out in prizes and 45% to education.

10/7/70

The press shills for legalized gambling, Rep. Wright Patman (D., Texas) contends. It gives the public "a steady diet of stories and pictures of winners—the big winners," he says, but "the poor soul who gambles away his family's rent money" is never publicized. Rep. Patman condemns the newly popular lotteries and off-track betting as "the most regressive" of all tax schemes. "It socks the poor and lets the rich—who do their gambling in stocks—off the hook."

7/14/71

Snake eyes: Over a decade, a California man traveled regularly to Las Vegas, where he took his lumps at the crap tables to the tune of $50,000 in losses. In 1967, when he won $1,300 but lost $10,000, he sought to soften the blow by deducting $1,230 in travel costs as expenses "for the production of income." A novel claim, the Tax Court said, and it considered it "long and hard." But at length it decided that no crapshooter with a record like his could really expect to turn a profit from the dice.

(Shiosaki v. Commissioner, T.C. Memo. 1971-24.)
2/10/71

A horseplayer failed to persuade the Tax Court he dropped $1,900 at the track. The only record of his bets was a list of which horse in each race was first out of the gate. This accurately reflected his system, the taxpayer claimed: An accomplice would signal which mount was away fastest, and he would scramble to lay a wager before the window slammed down on his fingers. "This form of proof is fraught with uncertainty," the court frowned.

(Zooloomian v. Commissioner, T.C. Memo. 1969-107.)
5/28/69

Pinball machines have enjoyed a $100,000 annual "subsidy" from Louisiana tax authorities, a watchdog group charges. The Public Affairs Research Council contends the state department of revenue doesn't collect a $100 tax on "gambling-type pinball machines." More than 2,000 such machines in Louisiana have been licensed by the IRS as gambling devices, but Louisiana taxes them at $50 as amusement devices, the council says. The revenue department has no comment.

5/13/70

Keeping Insurance Out of the Estate

A split Tax Court excludes a life insurance policy from estate taxes.

Unless overruled, the decision could greatly enhance life insurance as an estate-planning device. In the case, three children bought a policy covering their mother and at her death, collected $25,906. The mother, however, had paid all the premiums, totaling $4,821. Of that, it was conceded that $1,687—or about one-third—was paid "in contemplation of death." The IRS claimed that a like portion of the insurance proceeds should be taxed with her estate as a transfer in contemplation of death.

But the Tax Court ruled the woman never had an interest to transfer. From the first, her children owned the policy and all its benefits. "The focus," the court said, "must be on what (she) parted with as a result of her payment of the premiums. . . . The only thing diverted from her estate was the actual money paid." It counted only the $1,687 in her estate.

Four judges dissented. Realistically, the mother had bought the policy, one said. And the proceeds were the property created and transferred, not just the premiums.

(Estate of Coleman v. Commissioner, 52 T.C. No. 99.)
9/24/69

An Appeals Court excludes some life insurance proceeds from estate taxes.

The Fifth Circuit Court, the first appellate court to

rule on the issue, has reversed a district court and ruled against the IRS. The case involved two daughters who in 1953 each took out a $10,000 policy on their father's life. He and their mother paid the premiums, however, until his death eight years later. The IRS then claimed that the portion of the insurance proceeds attributable to premiums he paid in the last three years of his life should be included in his taxable estate as a transfer in contemplation of death.

The circuit court disagreed. It was unmoved by the IRS argument that the father had given his daughters insurance benefits, "a bundle of rights." The daughters already owned these rights, the court said, because they had taken out the policies. They could have paid the premiums as well, and their father's gift was simply the cash amount of the premiums he paid. An IRS ruling otherwise is "without support," the court said.

Because of a technicality, the court didn't rule on whether the premiums paid in the last three years became part of the estate. But the plaintiffs conceded they would have been.

(First National Bank of Midland v. U.S.A., U.S. Ct. of Appeals, 5th Cir., 1970.)
11/8/70

Taxing insurance: The IRS wins an important skirmish in a long battle.

If you give away an asset within three years before you die, your estate generally has to pay taxes on the asset as if you still owned it at death. When insurance is involved, applying this rule can get complicated. A wealthy person commonly will try to keep proceeds of insurance policies out of his estate by having someone else, say his wife or child, buy the policy, so the insured person himself doesn't own it. But often the insured still will pay the premiums himself. When all this happens within three years of death, thus bringing estate taxation of transferred assets into play, how much is taxable? There isn't much dispute that the premiums are. But courts have struggled to different conclusions on whether the proceeds of the policy are, too.

The Sixth Circuit appeals court has just ruled in one case that the full proceeds of a policy are taxable, even though the insured never technically owned the policy. A Michigan man had a trust buy a $100,000 policy on his life; the proceeds were payable to his children. He paid the initial premium, $9,600, and died six months later. His estate contended the only asset he gave away was the premium payment; the kids' trust owned the policy all along.

A district court agreed, but the Sixth Circuit in a two-to-one decision says the $100,000 also is part of the estate. In effect, the court held, the man wasn't giving away just the premiums but also the insurance protection the premiums bought.

(Detroit Bank & Trust Co. v. U.S.A., U.S. Ct. of Appeals, 6th Cir., 1972.)
9/20/72

A group life insurance policy can be given away, a U.S. court rules.

An insured man can often protect the proceeds of his life insurance from estate taxes by giving the policy to his wife or having her buy the insurance initially. This is frequent practice with policies individuals buy. Now the U.S. Court of Claims has upheld the transfer of a policy under a group life contract paid for by the insured's employer. The case involved the president and half-owner of a New York corporation who irrevocably assigned his $200,000 policy to his wife, also the beneficiary.

When the insured died, the IRS contested the transfer on the ground that he had kept "incidents of ownership," or control over the policy. For one thing, the IRS claimed, he could end his group coverage by quitting the company. But the court countered that the wife had acquired the usual right to convert group coverage into ordinary life. The tax men also argued the husband had control because by acting jointly with the other half-owner, he could cancel the company's group contract.

"A close question," the court said. But stock ownership wasn't enough. Proof was needed that an insured person held enough fellow holders in sway that he could end the contract at will. And this wasn't proved.

(Landorf v. U.S., U.S. Ct. of Claims, 1969.)
3/26/69

Another court decision upholds the assignment of group life insurance.

It's common for a person to exclude the proceeds of an individual life insurance policy from his taxable estate by assigning, or giving, the policy to someone else. The key is giving away "all the incidents of ownership." Now the practice is becoming more frequent with group life coverage, often paid for by an employer. The Tax Court recently upheld the transfer of two policies totaling $125,000 that a California man signed over to his wife.

One issue simply concerned the validity of policy endorsements permitting assignment. But the IRS also argued that California law bars giving away the right to convert the coverage to an individual policy. The Tax Court, however, found that right "just as much subject to assignment . . . as any other right."

The Revenue Service also objected that assignment could lead to a beneficiary who would suffer no financial loss if the insured died, and thus the policy would be void. Perhaps, the court said, but the possibility shouldn't prevent assignment.

(Estate of Gorby v. Commissioner, 53 T.C. No. 12.)
11/5/69

Interest grows in giving away group life insurance to avoid estate taxes.

This year some 15 states have passed laws authorizing the giving away, or assignment, of group life insurance policies. Others are considering such legislation. For years, insured persons have sheltered the proceeds of individual life policies from estate taxes by irrevocably assigning to someone else all the "incidents of ownership." These include the right to cancel the policy, borrow against it, or change the beneficiary.

Last year the IRS ruled that group coverage could also be assigned, where state laws and the group contract permit. Some insurance companies and business corporations report that the practice is growing. They note, however, that usually it's only worthwhile for those who have substantial coverage or more-than-moderate estates. (It's vital to give up the right to convert the policy to individual coverage. Otherwise, the insured could cancel his insurance by quitting his job.)

"It's a pretty serious step," one insurance official warns. "If you give your wife a $50,000 policy, and you happen to change wives, you're in trouble. The new wife gets nothing, you know."

7/9/69

The IRS drops a restriction on giving away group life insurance.

It has got much easier in recent years for a person to give away his interest in a group life insurance policy, thus keeping the proceeds out of his taxable estate. But it's essential to give up *all* control over the policy, including the right to convert it from group to individual coverage. If this right isn't relinquished, the IRS has reasoned, the insured retains some control because he has the power to terminate his coverage by quitting his job at the company where the policy is in effect.

Until recently, the IRS has held that in states where conversion to individual coverage isn't explicitly allowed, the policy can't be given away for tax purposes because of this job-quitting power to cut off the policy that the insured automatically retains. But the Revenue Service has reversed itself and ruled that this power alone doesn't constitute control over the policy if all other controls (such as the right to name beneficiaries) are given up.

(Rev. Ruling 72-307.)
6/28/72

A group life policy goes untaxed because the employer controlled key elements.

Sometimes insured persons will give up control over their life insurance coverage to keep the proceeds out of their taxable estate. Recently, however, the Tax Court decided a company-provided policy should be excluded because the employe didn't enjoy the "incidents of ownership" in the first place. His employer, Humble Oil & Refining Co., not only paid for the coverage, it also restricted eligible beneficiaries to the employe's spouse, children and parents, in that order.

The employe could specify whether his widow received the insurance in monthly payments or partly in such payments and partly in a lump sum. That struck the Tax Court as "very limited" say-so over the policy. The IRS claimed the employe also had the power to cancel the policy by quitting his job, but the court said that wasn't what Congress meant by "incidents of ownership."

The employe was authorized to assign his rights under the policy. But these rights were so meager that the power to assign them wasn't enough to bring the proceeds into his taxable estate, the court said.

(Estate of Lumpkin v. Commissioner, 56 T.C. No. 63.)
7/28/71

Of Interest and Debts

The IRS rules on when bank credit card charges are deductible as interest.

Not only did the ruling yesterday clear the way for taxpayers to deduct the full "finance charges" on bank cards like Master Charge or BankAmericard. The IRS also said "this same general rule" would apply to charge or credit customers of department stores. If it can be shown that no part of the "finance charge" is a carrying charge or other fee, then the entire charge is for the use of money and thus fully deductible as interest. (Otherwise a taxpayer can assume only 6%.)

Strictly speaking, it may be tough for a taxpayer to prove such finance charges are solely interest, but it's unlikely that the IRS will challenge such a conclusion. One important factor, the ruling indicates, is that the bank charges participating merchants a percentage of their credit card sales, and these fees are meant to cover all costs of the credit plan except interest. Thus the cardholder's charges must be interest.

The IRS also cites precedent that if borrower and lender agree "at arm's length in the loan contract" as to what portion of a charge is interest, that agreement "ordinarily" will be accepted for tax purposes.

(Rev. Ruling 71-98.)
2/3/71

Bache & Co. has its deductible interest cut because of its tax-exempt holdings.

Interest paid is normally deductible except when incurred "to purchase or carry" tax-exempt securities. In a case involving a partner at Bache & Co., a U.S. appeals court recently overruled the Tax Court and required that part of the firm's interest expense be allocated to the tax-exempt municipals it carried. Bache & Co. buys tax-exempts for resale, but during the period in question, these accounted for less than 1% of the firm's assets and gross income.

Bache borrows heavily from day to day, mainly to finance customers' margin purchases. The Tax Court said the borrowing wasn't undertaken to buy tax-exempts and ruled that Bache's interest costs were fully deductible. But the appeals court said no direct link to purchases of tax-exempts was necessary. It was enough that the firm took its intended purchases of municipals into account when determining its daily cash needs.

"Had Bache held no tax-exempts," the court said, "it would have had to borrow less." Thus, part of the interest—the court didn't say how much—wasn't deductible.

(Leslie v. Commissioner, U.S. Ct. of Appeals, 2nd Cir., 1969.)
7/30/69

An Irish Sweepstakes winner has a tax dodge thrown out as a sham.

In 1962, when a California couple won $140,000 in the sweeps, they looked around for shelter from the huge tax bite. They decided to buy a $168,000 apartment building, for which the owner asked $63,000 cash and assumption of a mortgage. The couple's accountant worked out a deal under which the seller kept the mortgage, but the couple paid him monthly instalments pegged at $3 more than the mortgage payments. This arrangement called for only $19,000 down—plus $44,000 as prepayment of five years' "interest" on the "debt."

The seller didn't care what the sum was called, as long as he got his $63,000 in cash. But the IRS balked when the couple deducted the $44,000 as interest. The Tax Court recently agreed. "No genuine debt was created to support the so-called 'interest' prepayment," it said. "The CPA merely juggled the figures."

But the court did permit the couple to deduct the $4,511 to the accountant for his tax advice and services.

(Collins v. Commissioner, 54 T.C. No. 163.)
9/9/70

Another winner in the Irish Sweepstakes goes through the Tax Court wringer.

The court recently set aside an apartment deal entered into by one sweeps winner. The court called it "a sham." Last week the court ruled on the business arrangements of another man who won $140,000 in the sweepstakes, and he lost on more points than he won. The man borrowed money to buy $210,000 in four-year Treasury notes, but the court disallowed deduction of $32,000 interest paid in advance. Interest isn't deductible on debts contracted solely to obtain a deduction, and the court found that was his sole intent.

The sweepstakes winner also bought 414 steers for fattening and resale. He claimed a $27,000 deduction for advance payments for feed, management services and interest on a mortgage. The court conceded that "the possibility of profit" was present, but it set aside $17,000 of the deduction. It said the sum wasn't clearly for a nonrefundable purchase of feed.

The court allowed him to deduct $15,000 paid New York State in income taxes, even though his actual tax bill came to $6,000. (The later refund was taxable income.) The $15,000 was what he would have owed, had none of his tax shelters held up.

(Estate of Cohen v. Commissioner, T.C. Memo. 1970-272.)
10/7/70

The tuition burden may be eased slightly by a new IRS ruling. It concerned a student who borrowed money under a student loan program to pay tuition, fees and other expenses. His father was required to co-sign the note, and as interest payments fell due, it was in fact the old man who paid them. Under these circumstances, the father was entitled to deduct the interest because co-signing the note made him liable for the debt.

(Rev. Ruling 71-179.)
1/21/71

A New Yorker claimed he made frequent gifts to family members by crediting accounts in their names carried by his firms as unsecured loans. He charged himself 10% interest on the unpaid sums, which was similarly credited. But the Tax Court denied his deductions of the interest "payments." Virtually no cash changed hands, it noted, and mere bookkeeping entries weren't actual gifts. Thus, no debts existed on which interest was due.

(Todd v. Commissioner, 51 T.C. No. 100.)
3/26/69

Salting a Little Something Away

The IRS spells out more detail on when pay can be deferred until retirement.

An employe can sometimes put off pay until later years, when he presumably is in a lower tax bracket. Generally, such an agreement must be made before the pay is earned, and the money can't be put aside in a special trust fund. In addition, the employer's duty to pay must merely be contractual, not covered by a note or otherwise secured.

The IRS recently outlined two specific circumstances that qualify. In one case, a firm gave annual bonuses to employes designated by a committee of directors. The committee had the sole right to defer any or all of the bonuses, and the employe had no right to the money until the deferral expired (a maximum of 10 years past retirement). In the other case, employes aged 40 or older could defer 5% or 10% of their salary. To take effect, the choice had to be made before a year began. The pay was paid over the 10 years after retirement.

In both instances, the IRS ruled that the pay wasn't taxable until the employe actually received it. Similarly, the company couldn't deduct the sums until actually paid.

(Rev. Ruling 69-649.)
1/14/70

Self-employed benefit plans leap in popularity.

IRS approvals of retirement plans set up by self-employed individuals soared to 66,400 in the first nine months of 1968, up from 29,400 for all of 1967 and 7,400 in 1966. The sudden allure: A change, effective in 1968, making annual contributions toward retirement fully deductible.

The law permits the self-employed to invest 10% of earned income, up to $2,500, under a regular retirement program. Interest and gains escape taxation until distributed. Until the deductible portion was boosted to 100% from 50%, applications lagged, largely because the self-employed must make equivalent payments for their own employes.

But some people run into problems with the plans. An osteopath, for example, bought $2,400 in U.S. retirement bonds in 1963, but didn't get around to submitting a plan for IRS approval until 1965. The Tax Court, ruling on his 1963 return, disallowed his deduction for the bonds that year on the ground that a definite written program must be in effect when contributions toward retirement are made.

A key point: Even though an IRS okay isn't essential to initiate a plan, some written program must exist to insure statutory requirements are being met.

2/5/69

Inept refunding can erase the tax benefits of pension plans, the IRS warns.

More self-employed persons are taking advantage of a law that lets them deduct 10% of their earned income, up to $2,500, and invest it under a tax-sheltered retirement program. But the law also provides that if the beneficiary taps the funds before he turns 59½, or is disabled, the money is subject to penalty taxes.

Recently one plan-holder was penalized when he cashed in an existing contract to put the proceeds into a new qualified pension plan. The transfer was a premature pay-out, the IRS ruled, because he wasn't legally obligated to put the money in the new plan. In other cases, the IRS noted, beneficiaries had avoided penalties. The trustee of one plan gave the money directly to the new plan's custodian. In another case, beneficiaries signed binding pacts to pay the money to their new pension trust.

(Rev. Ruling 69-254.)
6/4/69

It isn't enough for a pension plan to look good on paper, the IRS warns.

To qualify for special tax benefits, a retirement plan can't discriminate in favor of officers, shareholders or highly paid employes. Recently the IRS rejected a plan even though it treated everyone the same. It covered all employes, but provided that an employe forfeited his pension benefits unless he worked at least 15 years and stayed on until age 65.

Trouble was, the IRS said, except for a few stockholder-executives, all the employes were migrant workers, who in the nature of things never stayed around very long. The retirement plan might appear satisfactory on paper, but in operation it benefited only the brass.

(Rev. Ruling 71-263.)
6/30/71

Profit-sharing for salaried employes only wins approval by the Treasury.

Tax-sheltered profit-sharing plans aren't required to cover all employes, but they can't discriminate in favor of employes who are also officers, stockholders, supervisors or highly-paid. This has been a strict standard, but recently the IRS accepted a profit-sharing plan that included 40 salaried employes but excluded 110 others who would have qualified except for being paid on an hourly basis.

Those covered by the plan included four officers and 18 supervisors, many of whom were also stockholders. But the Treasury was willing to approve the plan as nondiscriminatory apparently because there was no great disparity between what the two groups were paid. Except for the top four officers, the pay of the salaried people was "substantially the same" as that of those on an hourly scale. One person on salary made less than $5,000, while 18 hourly wage workers made more than $15,000.

Some tax advisers interpret the ruling as a boon for small firms that employ skilled, highly paid craft workers but pay them on an hourly basis.

(Rev. Ruling 70-200.)
5/6/70

Profit-sharing at one small firm is rejected as stacked to favor its owner.

Company profit-sharing plans are allowed substantial tax benefits, but such plans can't discriminate in favor of employes who are officers, shareholders, supervisors or highly-paid. In one recent case, a small construction firm tied each employe's share of the firm's contributions to the length of his employment with the firm. The Tax Court ruled the plan discriminatory, however, because it resulted in a greater benefit for the firm's president-treasurer, who was also its sole shareholder.

The firm contended the provision served the legitimate end of encouraging employes to stay with the firm. The president happened to have been there longer than anyone else. But the court considered it irrelevant that the plan's objective was reasonable. If "invidious or rank discrimination" were required, that would substantially curtail the scope of the law, the court said.

Two judges dissented. They said the court's decision made it "virtually impossible" for a small, owner-operated business to set up profit-sharing tied to past service.

(McMenamy v. Commissioner, 54 T.C. No. 102.)
6/3/70

The pension plan at a small company failed to pass IRS muster.

The corporation had only two employes, the officer-shareholder and someone the IRS refers to as a "rank-and-file" employe. Its pension plan provided that the corporation contribute 20% of each employe's salary for the current year, or for his first year, whichever was higher. That sounds all right, but in practice it favored the boss.

The rank-and-filer earned $5,000, and under the plan, the corporation duly salted away $1,000 toward his or her pension. The officer-shareholder earned $50,000, but the annual contribution to his pension was $14,000, or 28%. That's because his first-year salary had been pegged at $70,000. The IRS ruled that this was discriminatory.

In effect, the plan was exploiting an IRS rule: If someone's pay is cut, there's no requirement that his pension benefits or contributions be cut back, too. But this provision can't be applied with discriminatory effect.

(Rev. Ruling 71-331.)
8/11/71

A gambler's choice is coming due for restricted stock granted after last June 30.

Restricted stock is a device to defer pay by allowing an employe to buy stock at a bargain rate, subject to forfeiture if certain conditions are violated (such as quitting his job before a given date). Formerly, no tax was paid until the restrictions lapsed.

The new tax law is much tougher: An employe will

incur an income tax when there is no longer "a substantial risk" of forfeiture. That tax would cover the spread between what he paid and the shares' market value when the tax comes due. Any subsequent appreciation is taxed as capital gain when realized.

But the law leaves an out for those who will take a chance. The employe can elect to pay the income tax the same year he receives the stock—even though real restrictions remain. This means that practically all appreciation is taxed at lower capital gains rates. But here's the catch: If the stock is forfeited, there's no refund or deduction for taxes already paid.

Normally an employe must make his choice within 30 days of receiving his stock.

(IRS News Release IR-1006, 1970.)
1/21/70

Sugar Ray wins a belated nod from the IRS on his deferral of income.

Some years ago, when Sugar Ray Robinson arranged to have a purse paid to him over several years, the IRS balked. It claimed the arrangement was a joint venture between Robinson and the boxing club, and Robinson's share was taxable when the club received it. But the Tax Court gave the decision to Robinson. Last week the IRS acquiesced and no longer lists the purse arrangement as an example of a joint venture.

In its place, however, the IRS offers the example of a theatrical performer who contracts with a producer to share the profits or losses from a play. The producer puts up the cash and does the things producers do. The performer takes the leading role, directs the play, and supervises other things. These facts amount to a joint venture, the IRS declares. The actor can't defer taxes on his share of the net, no matter when it is paid to him.

According to Tax Coordinator, an advisory service, the new ruling means that sharing profits in exchange for services may create a joint venture "where the individual also agrees to share losses."

(Rev. Ruling 70-435.)
9/2/70

No more rulings will be made by the IRS on the acceptability of pension programs set up by the self-employed under master or prototype plans. The service says it has already approved some 3,000 prototypes that the self-employed can adopt, and experience shows it's a waste of time to check each individual's program. The IRS will continue to rule on plans a person draws up himself, however.

(Rev. Procedure 69-24.)
11/12/69

The IRS eases rules on employe contributions to tax-sheltered company pension plans. An employe has been permitted to add up to 10% of his salary to employer contributions. But it's been assumed that if a full 10% wasn't salted away one year, it couldn't be made up later. Now, the IRS rules, payments may be made in any year, provided their total isn't more than 10% of total pay for all the years the employe takes part in the plan.

(Rev. Ruling 69-217.)
5/14/69

Pension plans that enjoy tax benefits can't discriminate in favor of officers, shareholders, or highly paid employes. The IRS nevertheless approved a plan under which most of the payout would go to the boss. The retirement pay was pegged at 50% of an employe's average career pay, and in the small corporation, the owner-officer's pay accounted for 80% of the payroll. The IRS didn't object, however, because the 50% rule applied to everyone.

(Rev. Ruling 71-255.)
6/23/71

When Doctors and Lawyers Incorporate

Doctors Inc. gains ground despite stubborn IRS opposition.

In California, it's estimated that some 30,000 doctors will choose to incorporate under regulations taking effect tomorrow. Lawyers are already eligible, and rules for dentists should follow in several weeks. At least 36 other states specifically permit such professional service corporations. In Oklahoma, a U.S. district court recently upheld an incorporated group of doctors. Federal tax collectors had previously lost all seven similar cases. Several are on appeal, and a Supreme Court test is likely.

"Taxes eat doctors to death," says Professional Financial Services Inc., Los Angeles. But a corporation of doctors can contribute up to 25% of employe salaries to pension and profit-sharing plans and deduct the payments as business expenses. The contributions aren't taxable to the doctors, and ultimate pay-outs are taxed as capital gains. One adviser figures that over 30 years, a doctor making $50,000 annually and saving 25% could accumulate $593,000 through a corporate plan, compared with $191,000 without a plan.

But some doctors object to increased bookkeeping and costs of incorporating. Other objections go deeper: "People are becoming more callous, more businesslike, but some older doctors feel incorporating is a loss of identity," an adviser notes.

4/9/69

Another circuit court blisters the IRS and upholds professional incorporating.

The stubborn IRS refusal to recognize corporations formed by doctors or other professionals as corporations for tax purposes appears battered and reeling. The Fifth Circuit appeals court recently upheld a Florida medical corporation. The court scored IRS rulings curbing incorporation as "wholly arbitrary and discriminatory . . . the only apparent expediency (they serve) has been the collection of more taxes." Being taxed as a corporation would make substantial tax benefits available to professionals.

The IRS says it hasn't decided whether to appeal the decision. One tax authority believes the taxmen are stymied. "They're gotten clobbered on this, and they're close to giving up," he predicts. To date, the Government has lost in three circuit courts and several district courts. With such agreement among lower courts, the tax authority maintains, the IRS isn't likely to obtain a Supreme Court hearing unless it can win at least one lower court to its side.

"They're finished," the tax expert declares. "The service is running out of circuit courts." (Indeed it was. The IRS abandoned its legal fight in August, 1969.)

(Kurzner v. U.S.A., U.S. Ct. of Appeals, 5th Cir., 1969, and IRS Technical Information Release No. 1019, Aug. 8, 1969.)
6/11/69

Professional corporations must be corporate in fact as well as form.

Last August, the Treasury dropped its protracted opposition to accepting professional service corporations as corporations for Federal tax purposes. Doctors in particular have been eager to gain tax benefits by incorporating. Now a Tax Court decision makes it clear that such benefits by no means follow automatically:

Such endeavors must "put flesh on the bones of the corporate skeleton."

The case involved four radiologists who set up a corporation under Wisconsin law. The men had separate practices in their own names before they incorporated, and their practices were largely unaffected thereafter —except that all their fees and expenses were paid into or from the corporation's checking accounts. Each doctor was credited with what he earned and docked for what he spent.

The Tax Court said the income couldn't be taxed to the corporation because it did nothing to earn it. It sold no services, owned no equipment, and exerted no real control over its "employes." "A mere set of bookkeeping entries and bank accounts," the court said.

(Roubik v. Commissioner, 53 T.C. No. 36.)
12/10/69

The Tax Court rules against a corporation it says was set up to avoid taxes.

Currently many professionals and other proprietors are on the brink of incorporation, attracted by likely tax advantages. But recently the Tax Court wouldn't permit a proprietor to gain by becoming an employe of his own business. The law provides that "amounts received under an accident or health plan for employes" are deductible by employers but don't count as income for employes.

A Wisconsin plumber incorporated to take advantage of this. Under a plan, the corporation would pay medical bills for full-time employes—of which he was the only one. In 1964, the business paid out $1,100. But the IRS argued the sum was taxable income for the plumber, and the Tax Court agreed. Though its decisions have wavered somewhat, the court has stressed that such medical plans must be "for employes." In this case it ruled the plan wouldn't benefit the plumber, as an employe, but rather as owner and sole stockholder.

"The genesis and the primary purpose of the plan —indeed of the incorporation—(was) the avoidance of Federal income taxation," the court declared.

(Smithback v. Commissioner, T.C. Memo. 1969-136.)
7/23/69

It may still pay for professionals to incorporate, Lybrand contends.

High Treasury officials have recently indicated that steps are afoot to equalize the retirement benefits permitted corporate employes and the self-employed. Maybe so, says Lybrand, Ross Bros. & Montgomery, the accounting firm, but such reports "shouldn't necessarily deter" doctors or other professionals from incorporating their practices. Lybrand says the Treasury has long discouraged such a move, and the latest reports may merely be "another attempt in the drive."

Lybrand contends it's impossible to predict when, if ever, such changes would become law. As yet, they aren't even formal proposals. Any effort to cut back current corporate benefit provisions will meet strong opposition, it says. If, on the other hand, self-employed benefits are liberalized to match current corporate benefits, incorporating may still be useful.

"Problems and pitfalls" will remain in setting up such corporations, Lybrand says, but these can be overcome. The latest Treasury ideas "don't alter the basic situation," the accounting firm concludes.

4/21/71

You Can't Take It With You

It gets harder to leave something to charity and postpone the gift.

When the wealthy make out their wills, they often set up what's known as a "charitable remainder" trust. This permits family or other beneficiaries to enjoy income from the estate during their lifetimes. After that, the remainder (the principal) goes to charity. This saves estate taxes because the estate gets an immediate deduction based on what the charity will eventually get. The Tax Reform Act set up stiff new rules for such trusts, but thousands of wills and estates remain under the old law.

These "old law" estates have been thrown into confusion of late. There's no deduction if the value of the eventual gift to charity can't be "readily ascertained." The Third Circuit appeals court shook things up last January when it overruled the Tax Court and denied a deduction. The appeals court said the trustee's powers were so broad that he could shortchange the charity in favor of the immediate beneficiaries. Thus the remainder couldn't be ascertained.

The Tax Court had ruled that the trustee's obligations under New York law were an adequate check on him, but the circuit court disagreed. Its decision has been appealed to the Supreme Court.

(Estate of Stewart v. Commissioner, U.S. Ct. of Appeals, 3rd Cir., 1971.)
8/11/71

IRS semantics over what's "necessary" in a trust don't impress the Tax Court.

You can give someone up to $3,000 a year without

being subject to gift tax, provided the gift is genuine and immediate, and not simply a future interest in property. Normally a gift in trust to a minor isn't considered a "future interest" if the money can be spent for the minor's benefit and the trust funds are turned over to him when he becomes 21.

Recently, however, the IRS challenged more than a score of trusts a wealthy Florida family set up for its children and grandchildren. Each trust agreement authorized the expenditure of income and principal "as may be necessary" for the education, comfort and support of the minor beneficiary. The IRS argued that the "may be necessary" phrase restricted the trustee's discretion to spend the funds and made the transfer a future interest.

The Tax Court disagreed. It found the wording "a gratuitous directive" that told the trustee to do what he had to do anyway: to decide what was necessary for the child's education, comfort and support.

(Heidrich et al. v. Commissioner, 55 T.C. No. 77.)
2/17/71

A tax break at death will live on despite recent congressional action.

Congress passed a law ending the long-standing provision under which certain Treasury bonds are redeemable at par for payment of estate taxes even though their current market value is well below their face value. The new law abolishes this tax break for bonds issued after March 3, but more than $40 billion of such issues are already outstanding and aren't affected. Their maturities range as late as 1998, so the tax device will take time to fade away.

Of course as dates of maturity draw nearer, the dollar difference between par and market value declines, and so does the tax saving. It will also be reduced if bond prices continue their recent rise. But attorney

A. L. Suwalsky Jr. of the Washington tax firm Silverstein & Mullens estimates that roughly $15 billion of the outstanding issues are selling low enough to consider buying with the estate tax saving in mind.

According to the attorney, the tax feature should remain attractive, at least to certain taxpayers, for another ten years.

3/24/71

Death and taxes: A person's taxable estate includes interests he transfers to others "in contemplation of death" within three years of dying, the law says. Thus, two $40,000 gifts an Oklahoma invalid gave her son and daughter two years before she died were taxed as part of her estate. But a district court disagrees. It held the daughter's gift—an interest in the parent's home—was mainly an inducement to move in and take care of her mother. The son got $40,000 because of a family tradition of giving the children equal gifts. Both gifts were motivated by "purposes associated with life rather than death," the court said.

(Stewart v. U.S., U.S. Dist. Ct., West. Dist. Okla., 1970.)
7/29/70

Two more cases lay to rest a particularly strained piece of IRS reasoning.

In one instance, a U.S. appeals court granted a widow's estate a deduction for a $68,000 coin collection left to the State of Israel. In another, the U.S. Court of Claims upheld a similar deduction for $275,000 left to a Bavarian town to build an old people's home. The IRS had opposed both deductions on the ground that if the law expressly permits an action, it bars a similar act if not explicitly allowed.

The law gives a deduction for bequests to a U.S. or state governmental body for a public purpose. Foreign governments aren't mentioned, so the IRS contends it follows that bequests to them aren't deductible. The IRS has stuck to that logic, even though another part of the law allows a deduction for bequests to trustees for a charitable purpose, without mention of any geographic limit. But the courts decided the coin collection and the old people's home were charitable purposes, and Israel and the Bavarian town could qualify as trustees.

"At best, the (IRS) argument is a highly technical contention," the Court of Claims said.

(Kaplun v. U.S.A., U.S. Ct. of Appeals, 2nd Cir., 1971, and National Savings & Trust Co. v. U.S.A., U.S. Ct. of Claims, 1971.)
2/24/71

The family farm survives an onslaught by the Internal Revenue Service.

Any time an elderly taxpayer makes a substantial gift, the IRS may challenge it as a subterfuge to avoid estate taxes. In one recent case, an elderly couple deeded over their 372-acre Texas farm to their four children and then leased it back under a sharecropping arrangement. Not long thereafter, health and financial problems cropped up, and the rent wasn't paid for four years. When the father died, his estate made up the payments.

The IRS insisted the gift wasn't valid because the parents kept an interest in the property. It also regarded the alleged "rent" as mere gifts to the children. But the Tax Court found nothing to suggest the lease was a sham. The parents were obligated to pay "a fair, customary rental" to the children, the court said, and "he who receives the rent in fact enjoys the property." True, the parents missed some payments, but that couldn't be foreseen, and it didn't mean they kept a right to the farm's income.

The father owed the back rent when he died, the

court said, so the estate was clearly entitled to a deduction for paying it.

(Estate of Barlow v. Commissioner, 55 T.C. No. 67.)
2/3/71

The Tax Court decided both an estate and the IRS were off base in valuing land.

Fixing a fair value on real estate for tax purposes has long been a thorny process, particularly when prices are rising rapidly. Usually the value is based on sales of comparable land in an area but even so, taxpayers and the IRS often wind up sharply at odds. In a recent estate case, an estate valued 170 acres of land in northern Delaware at $586 an acre, although property sales in the area around that time ranged from $1,000 to $2,600 an acre. The IRS said the estate land was worth $3,000 an acre. Subsequently, the estate raised its valuation to $1,000 an acre while the IRS came down to $2,000.

The Tax Court decided the value was $1,400 an acre after taking into account such things as the relation of sales of nearby land to the date of valuing the estate, whether such sales were for cash or on credit, the residential desirability of the land compared with nearby parcels and the topography of the various parcels.

The court rejected the IRS estimate because it was based on land that wasn't comparable and on mere offers to sell rather than actual prices. The estate's estimate wasn't accepted because it was based simply on the lowest sales price for land in the area.

(Estate of Mitchell v. Commissioner, T.C. Memo. 1968-297.)
1/15/69

A Dillon family trust is upheld in a complicated transaction.

In 1923, Mrs. Clarence Dillon set up a trust in which she kept a life interest in its income. Its corpus was to go to her husband if he survived her and to their children if he did not. In 1932, Mrs. Dillon created another trust to benefit their children, C. Douglas Dillon, later to become Secretary of the Treasury, and his sister.

In 1958, Clarence Dillon (acting through still another trust) turned over 72% of his interest in the 1923 trust to the 1932 trust. For this, the 1932 trust paid him $1.2 million.

Mrs. Dillon died in November, 1961. In the same month, the 1932 trust began to write off what it had paid Clarence Dillon for his life interest in the earlier trust. In 1962, it sought to deduct $198,000 from taxable trust income. The IRS denied $22,000 of the deduction, however. Part of the acquired life interest consisted of tax-exempt bonds, it said, and the cost of acquiring tax-exempt income shouldn't be deductible, it claimed. But the Tax Court ruled that acquiring a life estate wasn't subject to such a limit.

7/8/69

Small Business Matters

A corporate string slips through an IRS net.

The Treasury contends it was denied an estimated $235 million last year by some large enterprises that operate as a string of separate corporations to exploit a "surtax exemption" meant for small businesses. Corporations pay 22% on their first $25,000 of income, but 48% on earnings above that. One parent company on record had 516 subsidiaries, each claiming the lower rate on its first $25,000 earnings.

The IRS can bar multiple exemptions when corporations are set up mainly for tax ends. But one recent IRS effort was rebuffed. A New Yorker agreed to operate soft goods sections in six discount department stores. He created a corporation for each store. He chose that set up, he said, to limit his personal liability and keep the different operations separate. But the IRS scoffed. It noted he assumed unnecessary liability when he himself leased store space and borrowed money for the corporations.

The Tax Court ruled for the businessman. It found his rationale credible, even if not consistently followed. And facts indicated he didn't know of the tax advantages.

(Lake Textile Co. et al. v. Commissioner, T.C. Memo. 1969-44.)
3/19/69

A split Tax Court overturns an IRS ruling curbing Subchapter S corporations.

Subchapter S allows a small business to incorporate but be taxed as a partnership. Among other limits, such corporations are restricted to one class of stock. Sometimes, however, shareholders receive not only stock but notes for capital they put into the business. When most of a firm's assets are offset by such debt, the IRS feels the stock doesn't mean a lot, and the "debt" really shows ownership.

A California partnership formed such a corporation to operate a driving range. The new entity issued a total of 100 shares of $1 par stock to the former partners. It also gave them notes, bearing no interest, equal to the capital each had in the firm.

The IRS denied the firm qualified under Subchapter S. It cited a ruling that unless such debt is held "in substantially the same proportion" as the stock—and in this case it wasn't—the debt in effect is a second class of stock: It creates another set of ownership claims.

Over six dissents, the Tax Court held the ruling "invalid as applied to this case." Simple instalment debt, carrying no equity rights such as voting, didn't make another class of stock "merely because it creates disproportionate right . . . to the assets."

(Stinnett v. Commissioner, 54 T.C. No. 20.)
2/18/70

A small firm paid medical bills for its owner-operators, and a court approves.

People who run small businesses often aren't aware they can arrange to have their corporation pay their medical bills. Money received under an "accident or health plan for employes" isn't taxable income. A business may have different plans for different classes of employes, or leave out some entirely. It isn't even essential that the plan be in writing. The Tax Court recently upheld a plan limited to employes who were also officers —the couple who owned and ran a small supply house.

In 1965, their corporation paid $3,000 in medical bills for them. The IRS claimed the sum was taxable, but the Tax Court disagreed. By law, a plan must be "for employes," the court said, but employes could also be stockholders. The man and wife did most of the work; no excluded employe had comparable duties. There were a dozen lesser employes, but only one had worked more than four months. Their short tenure was "a natural basis" for exclusion.

And as the $3,000 qualified as a nontaxable benefit, it followed that the corporation could deduct it as a business expense.

(Smith v. Commissioner, T.C. Memo. 1970-243.)
9/2/70

Extra bonuses paid by a closely-held business survived court scrutiny.

The IRS objected when a plumbing contracting concern paid its president, the sole stockholder, and vice president, his son-in-law, bonuses totaling $175,000—more than twice the amounts formally authorized by the corporation's directors. (The two men, plus the president's wife, made up the board.) The payments were excessive, the IRS claimed, and therefore weren't deductible by the firm as a legitimate business expense.

The tax men's contention didn't fare well. The Tax Court found the bonuses reasonable in amount. And recently a U.S. Circuit Court also said that the lack of authorization by directors made no difference. The sole stockholder's action was binding on the corporation, it reasoned, because he had the only beneficial interest in the company.

And the IRS never objected, the court noted, in similar cases when bonuses paid were less than authorized amounts. Greater or lesser, the actual payouts were what mattered, the court said.

(L.R. Schmaus Co. v. Commissioner, U.S. Ct. of Appeals, 7th Cir., 1969.)
2/26/69

If You Live Abroad

Two Vietnam tours and no tax break: And what of the girl he left behind him?

April 15 hurts less for many Americans who live abroad. In 1967, some 91,000 claimed an exemption from U.S. tax for all or part of income they earned overseas (normally, the first $20,000). One way is to establish bona fide residence abroad for a full taxable year. But "bona fide residence" isn't always clear-cut.

An American signed on with an engineering firm to work in Vietnam. His contract provided that if he lasted 50 weeks, his return fare would be paid. He worked that long at a communications site at Pleiku, then returned to the U.S. He signed a new contract and was sent to Nha Trang. Some 13 months later, he left Vietnam for good. While in Vietnam, he enjoyed American officers' benefits, including commissary and PX. He became friendly with some Vietnamese, but spoke little of their language and read almost none. He acquired a motorcycle, a scooter and a Vietnamese "fiancee." At one point, he bought a house in her name.

The Court decided he had merely served two hitches, not become resident. On arrival, he apparently intended to stay 50 weeks, but not necessarily longer. He shared no "community of interest" with the Vietnamese, the court concluded. Nor was his pay subject to their tax.

(Coyle v. Commissioner, T.C. Memo. 1969-53.)
3/26/69

Jackpot! An itinerant "teacher" beats the one-armed bandits and the IRS too.

An American civilian spent six years traveling the

world from one American military club to another, hitting 500 in all. He made his way by "diagnosing and manipulating" slot machines, a skill he acquired while working for a firm that made slot machines. As he told it, he instructed GIs in his art, shared their jackpots, and helped them "beat the game of gambling itself, hence breaking addiction to it."

He claimed his take was tax-exempt as earned income from sources outside the U.S. But the IRS said he had rendered no service to "earn" it and socked him for $46,600 in back taxes. His "joint ventures" with GIs were just to get him in the club, it said. At first, the Tax Court agreed, but after a legal fight, it took a second look. He didn't have to render a service, it decided, as long as his income wasn't passive, like rental income.

When the IRS protested that gambling income isn't "earned," the court didn't disagree. But whatever the man was doing, he wasn't gambling, it said. It was the "diligent application of an unusual skill."

(Robida v. Commissioner, T.C. Memo. 1970-86.)
4/22/70

Love it or leave it—and your moving costs are deductible, the Tax Court says.

In late 1964, a chemical engineer and his wife packed up and left for Australia, immigrant visas in hand. He worked there about a year, but they soon returned to the U.S. On their 1964 return, they deducted $1,677 (the cost of moving down under) as unreimbursed moving expenses in connection with a new place of work. But the IRS denied the deduction. It said that expenses "allocable" to income earned abroad aren't deductible because the U.S. normally doesn't tax such income.

The engineer claimed the moving expenses were deductible because they were "personal in nature" and thus not allocable to what he earned in Australia. In a rare outcome, the taxpayer argued his own case and convinced the Tax Court over the dissenting views of five judges. The court's opinion said that until Congress changed the law, moving expenses were always seen as personal and nondeductible. And Congress didn't change their nature. It simply said that unreimbursed moving expenses could be deducted when incurred in connection with a new place of work.

The five dissenting judges said that if the engineer's outlays were connected with his new place of work, they were bound to be allocable to his Australian income.

(Hartung v. Commissioner, 55 T.C. No. 1.)
10/7/70

A new "loophole," more intriguing than important, may not be around long.

It concerns the new 10% minimum tax on preferences and its treatment of long-term capital gains. The Treasury has proposed regulations that suggest a taxpayer might escape the preference tax on gains by flying to the Bahamas and selling his assets there. That's because a capital gain from a foreign source isn't a "preference" unless it enjoys a preferential tax rate in the foreign land. In the Bahamas, capital gains are taxed the same as other income—that is, not at all.

That isn't preferential, the proposed regulations explicitly state. The liberal Treasury stance has Wall Street tax lawyers abuzz. Several startled attorneys say they consider it directly contrary to congressional intentions. Nevertheless, "a number of closings" have been switched to the Bahamas since the regulations came out. It's hard to get a law firm to say flatly that the Bahamian gambit will stand up in court. "What they say is take a chance," a lawyer explains. If it doesn't work, all it cost was a trip to the Bahamas.

The Treasury intends to revamp its proposed regulations shortly. The new version will say that if capital gains aren't taxed at all, that's "the ultimate preference."

6/2/71

Americans abroad may avoid most U.S. taxes even though the country they live in doesn't require them to pay its taxes, the Court of Claims rules. The case involved two professors sent to Argentina for the UN. Argentina granted them a tax-exemption and immunity from certain local laws. The court found that they had become "well integrated" in the Argentine community, and that was enough to qualify them as "bona fide foreign residents."

(Scott v. U.S., U.S. Ct. of Claims, 1970.)
11/4/70

And in Those Days . . .

There went out a decree from Caesar Augustus that all the world should be taxed.

So begins Luke's recounting of the birth of Christ, but his account has left Biblical scholars puzzled over exactly what levy Joseph returned to Bethlehem to pay. For centuries, Egypt had required a census of citizens every 14 years. Borrowing the idea, Caesar Augustus made a census mandatory in 6 B.C. (the presumed actual year of Christ's birth). It covered males over 14 years old and females over 12 and listed possessions and sources of income. The elderly were exempt.

Scholars aren't entirely sure, but they believe the taxes were imposed annually. It's clear they were steep. A Roman property tax in the provinces ran up to 25% to 33% of a crop's yield. It's known that the Romans also exacted a "poll tax," which included a uniform head tax, an income tax and other personal taxes. No one knows the exact rates, but they were steep, too. Taxes varied from place to place, often at the tax collector's whim.

The Jews came from well-defined families stemming from certain ancestral areas. To minimize tax evasion, the Romans ordered Jews to return to these places for the census. That's the reason Luke gives for having Mary and Joseph, who was of the House of David, travel some 60 miles by donkey from Nazareth to Bethlehem.

A few scholars question Luke's accuracy. They say the Manger story belongs in the same category as Jonah and the Whale. It should be read for theological, rather than historical, truth, they contend.

12/23/70

If you enjoyed this book,
you will also like . . .

OTHER TITLES FROM DOW JONES BOOKS

INVESTOR'S TAX SAVINGS GUIDE

by J. Crestol, H.M. Schneider & W.G. Wintrub
87 pages
Soft cover, $2.95

This highly sophisticated tax book covers all types of stock and bond transactions and how the new income tax law relates to them. Wash sales, short sales, puts and calls, commodity futures, trading expenses, income averaging, and more—all covered in this indispensable book that outlines ways of making trading work to the best "bottom line" advantage. 1970.

HOW TO SURVIVE A BEAR MARKET

by the Staff of Barron's
240 pages
Soft cover, $2.95

Third in the "How the Professionals Make Money Grow" series, adapted from "Talking Money," the popular articles on the question-and-answer sessions with the Barron's editors. Ten Wall Street professionals—insiders' insiders—present their views, which have a particular clarity that comes from being involved in the dynamics of the stock market on a day-to-day basis and from making the decisions that count. 1970.

FORTY YEARS ON WALL STREET

by George Shea
254 pages
Soft cover, $1.85 plus 15 cents postage
Hard cover, $5.50

Former financial editor of The Wall Street Journal, editor of Barron's, and author of "The Outlook," the well-known Journal column, Shea shares the most important lessons in a lifetime of "firing-line" experience on Wall Street. Here are the best of his Journal columns, ranging from the stock market to the many hazards of business forecasting. 1969.

THE DOW JONES INVESTOR'S HANDBOOK

edited by Maurice L. Farrell
120-140 pages, Soft cover

Convenient reference to stock and bond market indicators. Complete Dow Jones Averages through the end of the year prior to publication; individual records of common and preferred stocks listed on the New York and American Stock Exchanges (1969 edition on includes National Stock Exchange), showing the year's range of prices, net change, volume, and dividend, plus the year's most active issues; more than 2000 over-the-counter quotations (beginning in the 1970 edition); and articles of interest to the investor by the editors of The Wall Street Journal and Barron's

1968 edition, $1.85 + 15 cents postage
1969 edition, $2.45 + 15 cents postage
1970 edition, $2.60
1971 edition, $2.60

CHARLES H. DOW: ECONOMIST

edited by George W. Bishop, Jr.
307 pages
Hard cover, $9.50

A selection of his writings on business cycles. His editorials represent one of the earliest efforts to analyze the periodic ups and downs of the economy. The editorials collected, written around the turn of the century, illustrate the depth and calibre of Dow's work on business cycles. 1967.

DOW JONES AVERAGES WALL CHART

22½" x 27½", two colors
$2.95

The chart spans the past 50 years and shows monthly high-low fluctuations of the Dow Jones Industrial, Transportation and Utilities averages; and the volume of trading. Shipped rolled, ready for framing.

DOW JONES BOOKS, P.O. BOX 300, PRINCETON, NEW JERSEY 08540

TED WILLIAMS, SAM THE GENIUS and Other Sports Stories from The Wall Street Journal
192 pages
Soft cover, $1.95
There's a rumor among sports fans that the best sports writing in America can be found on the front page of The Wall Street Journal. That would be the last place a lot of sports fans would think to look, but to the Journal's three million readers, the talk isn't surprising. Some 30 of these stories, probing the business and human sides and the serious and funny moments in sports, are compiled here. 1970.

THE JILTED AARDVARK and Other Improbable Tales from The Wall Street Journal
110 pages
Soft cover, $1.95
Meant mainly to entertain, these 32 stories from the front page of The Journal include tales about the monkey that escaped in the airport; the poodle that didn't like his luxury doghouse; the stunt cyclist who can count to 20 before the anesthesia takes hold; Charles Atlas, who did have sand kicked in his face; and many more. 1970.

BUSINESS AND BLACKS
by the editors of The Wall Street Journal
150 pages
Soft cover, $1.95
This collection of articles from The Wall Street Journal relates the accomplishments and the disappointments in the attempts of the most important institutions in the country to "blend the racial minorities into the melting pot." What has been attempted, and how well? How have the minorities reacted? In short, how are things going? 1970.

OUR MISTREATED WORLD
by the editors of The Wall Street Journal
207 pages
Soft cover, $1.95
This is not a cheerful book. It is a collection of articles about how we have mistreated our physical world—how we have polluted its air and its rivers, littered its landscapes with junked cars and coal-mine waste heaps, slaughtered its wild creatures and threatened to destroy even ourselves with poisons of our own making. 1970.

LIVING DANGEROUSLY
by the Editors of The Wall Street Journal
104 pages
Soft cover, $1.95
This collection of Journal stories about men who risk death daily on their jobs seeks to explore not just how such individuals do their work, but why. You'll "experience" legendary rescues by an Alaskan bush pilot, the "combat" of a news cameraman, the feats of a scuba diver, a football linebacker, an auto racing driver, a rodeo cowboy, a mine sweeper, a police patrolman, and a "flying" ironworker who says "I like being able to do something that scares the hell out of other people." 1971.

RIDING THE PENNSY TO RUIN
by the Editors of The Wall Street Journal
90 pages
Soft cover, $1.95
In 1970, the answer to all railroading problems—the Penn Central—filed for reorganization under the bankruptcy act. This is a collection of twelve Journal articles written between June 1970 and April 1971, relating the fascinating stories of government involvement, questionable stock transactions, outmoded equipment and work rules, "lost" freight cars, and more, involved in one of the biggest single financial disasters in history. 1971.

DOW JONES BOOKS, P.O. BOX 300, PRINCETON, NEW JERSEY 08540